the origins *of* fruit *&* vegetables

jonathan roberts

the origins *of* fruit *&* vegetables

UNIVERSE

First published in the United States of America in 2001
by UNIVERSE PUBLISHING
A Division of Rizzoli International Publications, Inc.
300 Park Avenue South
New York, NY 10010

2001 2002 2003 2004 2005 2006 / 10 9 8 7 6 5 4 3 2 1

Printed in China by Midas Printing Ltd

ISBN: 0-7893-0656-5

Library of Congress Control Number: 2001094245

Contents

**BOTANICAL
ENGRAVING OF
THE FIG, PLATE 73**
JOHANN JAKOB HAID
1704–1767
Private Collection

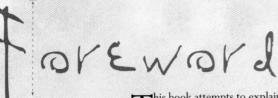

Foreword

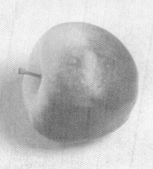

This book attempts to explain how, when and where the vegetables and fruit that we drop, net-bagged or cellophaned, into our shopping carts evolved from their wild ancestors: to tell their story, as it were, *sub specie aeternitatis*: within the context of eternity.

The flowering plants go back a very long way, to perhaps one hundred million years before anything resembling a human being ever shambled across this planet. Their story passes via the seed ferns, the trees of the ancient tropical forest and land-usurping seaweeds, to the single cell organisms that slurped about in the primal, soupy seas of our newly created world.

As one who finds difficulty in remembering the names of his own daughters, let alone the Latin names of plants, it is always a comfort to me to remember that all living things—trees, butterflies, humans and kangaroos—descend from these simple, nameless protoorganisms from four or five billion years ago.

The genesis of this book can be fairly precisely dated: to an autumn afternoon two years ago when our local archaeological society came to visit the Roman hill-fort above my West Dorset home. If barrack foundations were anything to go by, it housed a lot of soldiers. How were they supplied? By boat from Gaul? We stood in a group on the hilltop and looked out over the coombs undulating down towards Bridport, Golden Cap and Lyme Regis and tried to imagine an unbroken, wild wood rug of trees before colonization into fields and farms, and an island population of perhaps a million Britons at the most. "What did they do for fruit and veg?" someone wondered. A simple, intriguing question to which I resolved to try and find the answer. This book is the result of my research.

The evolutionary careers of fruit and vegetables can be adumbrated, in some cases, long before human history begins: of the avocado, for example, whose *Persea* genus is thought to have rafted across the Atlantic on North America when the supercontinents, Laurasia and Gondwana, broke up and drifted apart; or of the strawberry, herbaceous descendant of the shrubby, thuggish blackberry—consider the similar way in which their suckers arch over and root where they make contact with the earth. But my accounts begin, mostly, with the advent of man: first as a hunter tasting and testing leaves, roots, seeds and fruits in the wilderness; then perhaps as a hut or cave dweller with edible plants growing conveniently, as if by magic, on the midden outside his door; as a cultivator sowing seeds in garden plots and selecting chance mutants or hybrids for improved size, taste or yield; finally as a breeder, deliberately hybridizing—or, more recently, altering genomes—to produce a "superior phenotype."

Mutant frequency in plants is about 1:50,000, and the vast, variant majority are born to blush unseen and waste their sweetness. The creation of new plants, by natural speciation within niches, can be aeon-slow. The new science revealed by the discovery of DNA, on the other hand, has two astonishing faculties. Quite apart from its ability to produce bespoke plants to order, it can vastly accelerate the evolutionary process of species creation at a time when species loss throughout the planet is occurring at an alarming rate and, as botanists gradually extend their DNA profiles of plants, ancestral maps of core species in the distant past can be plotted with some precision.

A major fascination, for me, has consisted in tracing how a wild plant in one part of the world turned into a successful, domesticated fruit or vegetable in another: the chili pepper of Peru travelling to Hungary in the seventeenth century to become an immediate hit; the Asian shaddock metamorphosing into the Florida grapefruit; strawberry species from North and Latin America hybridizing in eighteenth-century northern France, to create the delicious pineapple strawberry that we eat today with sugar and cream.

To all those who have helped me in researching and writing this book, I extend my thanks. The list is long, a roll call would be invidious. I make an exception in the case of my wife, Annie, whose patient encouragement has seen me across some rough ground, and to whom this book is most gratefully dedicated.

Further reading

The standard technical work on the subject is *Evolution of Crop Plants*, edited by Smartt and Simmonds (second edition, 1995). It is a collection of essays by plant experts from all over the world, and covers most, and many more, of the plants in my list. It remains, though, to the layman, a fairly inaccessible read. *Domestication of Plants in the Old World* by Zohary and Hopf (1994), provides an excellent, up-to-date overview of the archaeological evidence for plant domestication in the Mediterranean basin and the Fertile Crescent. Alphonse de Candolle, in his classic *Origine des Plantes Cultivées* (1882), traced most of the more important cultivated plants back to wild species by systematic and rigorous comparison of old with new; work that was extended by the great Russian botanist, Nikolai Vavilov (*Cultivated Plants*, 1951) who led expeditions all over the world between the two World Wars to identify the primary gene centers of cultivated plants in the wild.

For those in search of a longer, and wider, view of plant evolution, E.J.H. Corner's *The Natural History of Plants* (1966) is a wonderfully evocative account of how cells, free-swimming in the ocean, became attached to make seaweeds, and how seaweeds elongated their cells and formed lignin to make trees on land, with roots and branches and photosynthesizing leaves. Corner was a Cambridge mycologist who became fascinated by tropical rain forests—palm trees in particular—and worked in the field in Latin America and southeast Asia. His inspiration was a thin little book, published in 1919 by A.H. Church, with the rather beautiful title *Thalassiophyta and the Subaerial Transmigration*. It begins famously: "The beginnings of botany are in the sea . . ."

fruit

"On the outside of the courtyard and next to the doors is his orchard, a great one, four land measures, with a fence driven all around it, and there is the place where his fruit trees are grown tall and flourishing, pear trees and pomegranate trees and apples trees with their shining fruit, and the sweet fig trees and the flourishing olive. Never is the fruit spoiled on these, never does it give out, neither in winter time nor summer, but always the West Wind blowing on the fruits brings some to ripeness while he starts others. Pear matures on pear in that place, apple on apple, grape cluster on grape cluster, fig upon fig."

STILL LIFE WITH
PEACHES AND
GRAPES, 1636
LOUISE MOILLON
1610–1696
Private Collection

THE ODYSSEY VII, 225 FF. Description of the fabulous gardens of Alkinous, king of the Phaeacians, by Homer, epic poet of Greece. Homer lived and sang around 900 B.C.

Avocado Persea americana *of the* Laurel *family*

The avocado is the world's most nutritious fruit. It belongs to the *Persea* genus of the *Lauraceae* or Laurel, a fairly large (forty-five genera and over 1,000 species), mainly tropical or subtropical family of trees and shrubs that includes the bay laurel and cinnamon tree; a family readily identifiable by the aromatic oil contained by all its members.

Persea began its career in the ancient African forest many millions of years ago, at the time and from the place where the angiosperms, the flowering plants, are thought to have set out to colonise the planet. By the time of the European voyages of discovery in the fourteenth and fifteenth centuries, *Persea* was extinct in Africa—yet it was growing contentedly in the Americas and in southeast Asia. A Robinson Crusoe of an evergreen woodland tree, *Persea indica*, was found by early European sailors—it still survives—in the Canary Islands. How is this possible?

Rather neatly, *Persea* illuminates the theory of continental drift first proposed by the German meteorologist Alfred Wegener in 1912, and gives us some inkling of how plants rafted, or island-hopped, from one side of the world to the other as the two supercontinents, Laurasia and Gondwana, broke up and moved.

The story goes something like this. About one hundred million years ago the flowering plants—and *Persea*—evolved from a group of seed ferns in what is now the West African part of Gondwana, which at that date included South America, Antartica, Africa, India and Australia in one vast continent. *Persea* then migrated—and speciated—north across the Spanish land bridge into Laurasia (North America, Europe and Asia). Some of its species sailed west across the Atlantic on North America when she emigrated from Europe; others turned east and traveled overland to Asia. At the same time a primitive *Persea* split off to become the subgenus *Eriodaphne*, a domestic in Gondwana, and was enjoying a slow raft ride west on South America, or hopping between islands left behind in her wake.

Thirty-five million years later, at the end of the Cretaceous period, when the continents had more or less settled (but the Central American Land Bridge had not yet surfaced), *Eriodaphne* was well-established in niches in South America, while *Persea* was rooted in North America, and the lauraceous forests of Africa whence they had emerged had been utterly extinguished by climate change.

This explains why fifty- to sixty-million-year-old fossils of *Persea* (a tropical plant) have been found in temperate Europe (tropical then) and in the bitter cold winter uplands of Montana in the U.S. It also clarifies why the *Persea* species from North America and southeast Asia can still interbreed, but crosses between *Persea* and *Eriodaphne* (who divorced at a much earlier date) are invariably infertile.

So where did *Persea* plants that we would recognise as avocados first grow? It is hard to be sure, but the area north of Mexico City is considered the likeliest centre of origin. It has long been accepted that avocados divide botanically into three main subspecies: the Mexican or subtropical Highland, which can tolerate some frost and likes elevations, in the torrid zone of the tropics, from 5,000ft to 10,000ft; the Guatemalan or semi-tropical, which grows from 3,300ft to 6,600ft and is less frost-resistant; and the tropical Lowland or West Indian, which prefers sea level and is tolerant of salt spray (all three hate wind and demand windbreaks: branches are brittle and roots shallow). A likely scenario is that the Mexican subspecies was the protoparent.

Following the rise of the Central American Land Bridge about six million years ago, its seed was spread to Guatemala and El Salvador (on whose Pacific coast it adapted to tropical, low-level niches) by large, fruit-eating birds, or by animals like the mastodon and giant ground sloth. These creatures that are known to have roamed Central America as recently as ten thousand years ago, would have passed big avocado seeds through their digestive systems without blinking their prehistoric eyes.

There is evidence from carbon dating that avocados were being gathered by humans in the Mexican uplands around 8,000 B.C. and were being cultivated about 1,000 years later. Superior genotypes were also being selected and planted by men as early as 6,000 B.C. (avocados have the advantage of growing true, and germinating easily, from seed).

When Hernando Cortes landed in Mexico in March 1519, he found the Aztec Indians, who had never seen a cow, sheep, goat or

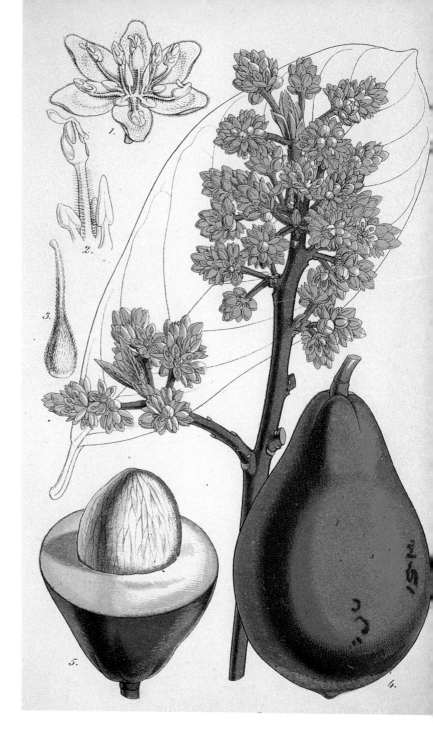

**EQUADORIAN
INDIANS IN FINE
COSTUMES**

VICENTE ALBAN
EIGHTEENTH CENTURY

*Oil on wood panel
Museo de América
Madrid, Spain*

horse, growing and eating calorie-rich avocados to supplement their diet of turkey, dog, fish, rabbit or maguey slug—and their avocado cultivars probably were not that very much different from kinds of varieties that we grow today. They called the avocado *ahuacatl* (the Inca name in Peru was *palta*) and they relished it then, as they still do. The Indians of Guatemala say, "four or five tortillas, an avocado and a cup of coffee—this is a good meal." They are quite right too: the avocado is good for you—especially if you are a diabetic. It is a high-energy food that is low in sugar, full of vitamins, especially A, B and E, and a useful source of soluble and insoluble fiber. It is particularly good as a first solid food for babies, and, because its fats are monounsaturated, doctors recommend it for

A... *Yndia en trage de Gala.*
B... *Yndia del Canpo con su Paba Real.*
C... *Arbol de Aguacates, y su Fruta.*
D... *Arbol de chihuacanes con su Fruta entera, y partida.*
E... *Arbol de Chamburos con su Fruta entera, y abierta.*
F... *Mamey con sus ojas, y Fruta abierta.*

bad hearts. Then, as now, it was eaten raw, straight out of the skin.

El Capitān Gonzalo Fernandez de Oviedo y Valdés, to give him his full title, was a Spanish *caballero* who landed at Panama's Darien in 1513 and spent thirty-four years in different parts of the Spanish Main. His *Historía Général y Natural de las Indias*, published in 1526, was the first ever serious attempt to describe the fauna and flora of the New World. In it he wrote appreciatively and at first hand of the Central American berry, the avocado, which he called in his own tongue, following the Aztec, *ahuacate* (later corrupted to *abuacado* in Spain, *aguacate* in Latin America, *avocado* in Italy, *avocatier* in France and *avokado* in Russia). He wrote, "the part which is eaten is a paste similar to butter and of a very good taste."

In the early years following the discovery of the New World, however, once the excitement of not finding black pepper had died down, the Spanish colonists were much more interested in importing and growing crops and fruit from the Old World rather than experimenting with buttery plants indigenous to the New. It was nearly one hundred years (1601) before avocados—the seeds, not the fruits, travel well—began to be grown in southern Spain.

The avocados arrived in Jamaica in 1650, in Mauritius by 1780 and in Asia by 1850. They were first recorded in Florida in 1833 and in California (the area now second behind Mexico in the world production league) in 1836. The Mexican highland avocado subspecies, pear-shaped, smooth-skinned and resistant to cold, was the type most commonly grown in Europe and California, but fruit sizes tended to remain disappointingly small and consumers outside the growing countries, before the days of fast air transport, remained less than ecstatic about the perishable fruit. The fleshier, fattier, rougher skinned cultivars— hence the old name "alligator pear"— obstinately refused to fruit, or even to grow, outside the tropics.

Then in 1911 an American grower in Mexico discovered a Mexican x Guatemalan shiny green, pear-shaped hybrid that was resistant to cold, weighed in at a decent 8–14oz and had a high oil content (eighteen to twenty-six percent). He called it Fuerte and it soon became the world's most popular cultivar. In recent years, Hass, which occurred as a chance seedling in California, has joined it in pole position. It is of the Guatemalan race, with a ten percent addition of Mexican genes making it mature earlier and more frost-tolerant.

Both types are grown in California, and in Israel and Cyprus, the leading producers of the Mediterranean basin. Mature fruits can be left on the trees for several weeks, but picking is a tricky, time-consuming business. Because avocado branches are so brittle, pickers can not climb into the trees, but use sacks and rope-operated knives on the end of long poles to cut the fruits down, one by one, for packing in boxes. In the past all attempts by breeders to hybridise the two subgenera by cross-pollination has failed; but if the *Eriodaphne* gene that gives resistance to the foot rot fungus, *Phytophthora cinnamomi*, could be copied and inserted into *Persea americana* . . . ? A genetic marriage between the two plants, disrupted so many millions of years ago, may soon be arranged.

Blackberry, raspberry, loganberry, wineberry, & cloudberry

Rubus genus of the Rose family

The Blackberry is a primitive thug that has been turning parts of the northern hemisphere into off-limit areas since well before the last Ice Age began, some thirty-five thousand years ago.

In late summer, watch the horror movie way its sprays search with their tips for somewhere to sucker and root. Raspberries progress underground about 6.6ft a year and, like mushroom fairy rings, use up the available food supplies in their wake. Blackberries reach out farther and quicker, arching through the air. Introduced to New Zealand in the nineteenth century, they quickly became one of the country's worst weeds. Kiwis' joke that there are two species of blackberry in the country now: one strangling the North Island, the other the South.

With a character so disagreeable, it is little wonder that the blackberry was turned away from the garden gate until very late—until the early 1800s, in fact. It is good for jams, the roots give an orange dye and the leaves are said to help burns and swellings. But what is the point of cultivating it, when one can pick it so easily in the wild?

It has been gathered by humans since well before historic time, having colonized almost all the cooler, more temperate parts of the northern hemisphere. In fact, it detests the tropics from which it once emerged

northwards as an aggressive, hardy, colonizing shrub, and rarely occurs south of the equator as a true native. It was helped on its way by tree-felling humans: cut a clearing in a wood and watch the brambles grow.

Seed pips of the European blackberry, growing wild throughout Europe and western Asia, have been found in interglacial and medieval contexts throughout Europe. This includes inside the stomach of a human, probably from Neolithic times, which was dug out of the Essex clays near Walton-on-the-Naze in 1911. Blackberry seeds are quite easy for archaeologists to identify, having a characteristic diamond-paned window surface pattern; they are distinguishable from kidney-shaped raspberry seeds, being bigger—up to .11in long—and rounder.

Sorting out the ancestral pedigree of blackberries is a bit of nightmare for botanists. There are over three hundred wild species in Europe alone and, like cabbages, they are polymorphic plants, able to hybridize and assume a wide variety of forms depending on factors like climate and soil. Their sexual reproductive system is very complex: in some

INTERIOR SCENE,
1948 *(opposite)*

LUCIAN FREUD
B. 1922
Pastel on paper
Private Collection

aboriginal species, the ability to reproduce themselves sexually with pollinated seeds is more or less complete, but other polyploidal species (having several chains of chromosomes) are "apomictic"—they can only produce asexual seeds and reproduce only by cloning.

The two primary ancestor species of the cultivated European blackberry are thought to be *R. tomentosus* and *R. ulmifolius*. Both are still widely distributed in Europe and west Asia; they are diploid plants (having two chains of chromosomes, un multiplied by hybridization). *Tomentosus* has upright stems covered with hooked thorns, white-to-pink flowers and round fruits. *Ulmifolius* has pink flowers, long curved thorns only on stem angles, felted undersides to its leaves and egg-shaped fruits. It is considered the best-tasting of the European wild blackberries. In the U.S., two types have been taken into cultivation: the erect eastern American blackberries that derive from another diploid, *R. allagheniensis*, which has stout, straight prickles, white flowers, and sweet round fruit; and the trailing western American blackberries or "Californian dewberries," long separated from their cousins by the Great Plains and the Rocky Mountains. They are complex, polyploidal plants, with high chromosome numbers (fifty-six and eighty-four), which suggest a prolonged mishmash of evolutionary activity— hybridization, mainly, involving a number of diploid plants. *R. ursinus*, the Californian dewberry, has trailing stems, straight prickles, white flowers, and black, usually oblong fruit.

The Greeks and Romans were well acquainted with blackberries. Ovid, in his *Metamorphoses*, written during the first decade

of the Christian era just before he was banished by the emperor Augustus to Tomi on the Danube, harked back to a Golden Age when men were content with wild foods. "They gathered arbutus berries and wild strawberries, wild cherries and blackberries that cling to thorny bramble bushes." A generation later, Pliny the Elder claimed that the arching sprays of blackberry had inspired man to propagate plants by layering. Its berries were astringent (good for diarrhea), he wrote, and soothed sore gums and tonsils.

Throughout the Dark and Middle Ages, the blackberry retained its status as a gathered, nuritious fruit, while never quite ridding itself of disreputable, perhaps even sinister, connections. It was widely believed in medieval England that, around Michaelmas, the Devil spat or urinated on blackberries, making them unfit to eat. Graves in churchyards were tangled with brambles, to keep ghosts in their coffins. On the principle of treating like with like, it was believed that diseases could be cured by passing a sufferer

brd and Dispopled be layse And holy god toke therof gret vengeaunce vpon hem that Did the fete iske aftir othir.

St Albans'

Chronicle *(above right)*

late fifteenth century

Blackberries illuminate an illustration of Robert Marmion, despoiler of the Church during King Stephen's reign, who dies falling from his horse. Lambeth Palace Library, London, U.K.

Pliny the Elder

Gaius Plinius Secundus

Roman scientist and scholar, lived from A.D. *23–79*

Etching from Savants de l'Antiquité

J. Hayllar.
Oct 1872

beneath a bramble arch that was rooted at either end. In some English counties blackberries were known as "scaldberries": it was supposed that children who ate too many contracted "scald-head," a disease of the scalp.

Geoffrey Grigson, in his *Englishman's Flora*, tells the old story, probably Elizabethan, of the cormorant who went into partnership with a bat and a bramble to ship sheep's wool overseas. Their boat sank—and that is why the cormorant is always diving, looking for the wool; why the bat comes out only at night, to avoid its creditors; and why the bramble steals wool from sheep, to recoup its losses.

It was in America, at the beginning of the nineteenth century, that blackberries were first brought into cultivation. Before 1829, when *The New York Gardener* tentatively suggested their domestication, the only references to them in American horticultural literature were how to get rid of them.

The first commercial scale plantings were made by Captain J. Lovett of Beverley, Massachusetts in 1835. He used eastern American erect blackberries, without huge success. But growers experimented and by 1867, eighteen cultivars were listed, including the Oregon Evergreen Black, or Cutleaf blackberry, *R. laciniatus*, which originated in central Europe. The Cutleaf arrived in the New World by a roundabout route: a wild plant was dug up on Walton Heath in Surrey, taken to a South Sea island by a settler, then transported on to Oregon by a Frenchman. In 1930 a thornless mutant of *laciniatus* was found growing in the wild and became a bestselling cultivar.

In the early 1890s, the American nurseryman Luther Burbank trumpeted his new Himalaya Giant blackberry as originating "high up in the Himalayan mountains"; in fact, it was *R. procerus*, which grows wild in southern Europe; it is a rampant, vigorous, heavy-cropping blackberry that will take over the average garden in a matter of weeks.

Today, the blackberry remains a secondary crop in Europe, but in America, particularly in Oregon, and in New Zealand, it is farmed on a fairly large scale. In the last thirty years cultivars have been bred—particularly from the western American blackberries—which have an excellent flavor, ripen earlier, and yield more.

The loganberry, although a hybrid, has been given species status as *R. loganobaccus*. Its origin is well-attested, by no less an authority than Judge J H Logan of Santa Cruz, California, who invented it in 1881. He grew a western American trailing blackberry, *R. ursinus* (Californian dewberry, which has oblong fruits) next door to a forty-year-old red raspberry with hemispherical fruits (probably a variety called Red Antwerp), and grew about one hundred plants from seed gathered from the blackberry. They fruited in 1883, and one of them, a hybrid cross between the two plants, was the loganberry that we all now grow in our gardens. It was introduced to Europe in about 1887.

The red raspberry, *Rubus idaeus*, has grown wild throughout northern Europe and Asia since well before historic time. Two other species, one red-fruited, *R. strigosus,* and the other black-fruited, *R.*

October, (From a Series of Twelve)

(opposite)

Jessica Hayllar
1858–1940

*Julian Simon Fine Art Ltd
London, U.K.*

Loganberry jam

occidentalis, both native plants to North America, have equally ancient origins. *Occidentalis* tends to have a more southerly range—into Colorado—than *strigosus*, which stops farther north in Wyoming.

Raspberry seeds have turned up in late glacial deposits on the Channel coast and in Scotland—now a premier area for their cultivation in the northern hemisphere—at a site at Bundsø in Denmark that dates from the third millenium B.C. and in Bronze Age and Roman sites in northern Europe. Like the blackberry, it proved just as adept at colonizing forest clearings and disturbed land and seems to have been gathered by humans for many thousands of years before being brought into cultivation.

The Greeks and Romans seem to have used the plant more for medicine than eating. The elder Pliny, who called it the Ida Bramble—

there was a legend that it originated on Mount Ida in Asia Minor—recommended its blossoms as a salve for sore eyes and, soaked in water, for stomach troubles. By the fourth century A.D., when Palladius wrote his long poem *De Re Rustica*, it was being grown in gardens in Italy. It failed to get a mention either in Charlemagne's ninth-century list of cultivated plants or in the fourteenth-century *Forme of Cury* that itemized English fruit and vegetables, although that does not necessarily mean that medieval monks, who knew their Pliny and Palladius, were excluding it from their gardens. The first mention of the raspberry in English is in Turner's 1568 *Herbal*. He called it *Raspis* and said that it grew

in the greate highe hills a little above Bone and in East Friesland in a wood besyde Anrik and in many gardines of England. It hath much shorter stalkes then the bramble and no great howky prickles.

He repeated Pliny's medicinal recipes, adding that "raspis wine," made from juice of the berries, was good for stomach and gums. Since about the fifteenth century the English had imported from France a sweet, dark-red grape wine they called "respyce" or "raspis" that would have resembled raspberry juice.

Gerard illustrated both the blackberry and the "raspi'" in his 1597 *Herball*, and, as usual, his information was wrong. "The raspis," he wrote, "is planted in gardens; it groweth not

Rubus odoratus   Sweet Canada Raspberry

RASPBERRY, SWEET CANADA
from The British Herbal
by John Edwards
1763–1812
British Library, London, U.K.

THE CLOUDBERRY
(*R. CHAMAEMORUS*)
THE THOMAS BOLTON
COLLECTION
Natural History Museum
London, U.K.

wilde that I know of, except in the fielde by a village in Lancashire called Harwood, not farre from Blackbushe."

In Gerard's time and in northern Europe, the raspberry was still regarded primarily as a medicinal plant. Raspberry leaf tea, made by infusing one ounce of dried leaves in a pint of water was, and still is, very good for diarrhea, as a gargle for sore throats, and as a salve for wounds and burns.

As the new ideas of the Renaissance were diffused and as consumers slowly lost their medieval apprehensions about fresh fruit, gardeners began improving raspberries for eating, selecting cultivars with fewer, stronger canes and bigger fruit. Parkinson, in 1629 mentions two varieties, red and white, and Worlidge's 1678 *Vinetum Britannicum* lists three: the Common Wild, the Large Red Garden, and the White (whose fruit is, in fact, yellow not white).

Cultivars producing larger fruit were arriving in western Europe about this time from Hungary and the Balkans. By the end of the eighteenth century, the culture of raspberries was well understood and varieties like Yellow Antwerp, first grown in England by Lord Middleton who brought it from Hungary via Antwerp, were making an impact. In 1806 William Forsyth, the London gardener for George III and George IV, listed eight cultivars and twenty years later the Horticultural Society—it became the Royal Horticultural Society in 1861—recommended twenty-three.

European raspberry canes sailed the Atlantic with New World settlers in the sixteenh century; their fruits seem to have been

preferred to the native American blacks and reds, which were not brought into cultivation until much later—well into the 1800s. But the best crosses occurred, mostly by chance, between red raspberries from the two continents. Old World species contributed good fruit quality, New World species added tolerance to heat, cold and drought.

Their hybrids showed the hybrid vigor that Darwin, among others, helped to discover. Cuthbert was found growing in a New York garden in 1865, Preussen in Germany in 1915: both became world famous cultivars for growers and breeders. Lloyd George, a chance seedling discovered in a Kentish wood and first distributed in 1919, proved immensely popular in its day. But new cultivars tended to deteriorate quickly in yield and vigor, mostly as a result of infection by virus and other diseases.

In the 1980s, for instance, plantations throughout the world were devastated by *Phytophthora fragariae* var. *rubus*, which attacks raspberry root systems. Breeders have had to run hard to stand still: finding varieties bred from virus-free stocks that can cope with modern diseases. The new GM technology has, on the whole, been given a cordial welcome by raspberry breeders, in America anyway. Biotechnicians are able to transfer cowpea tripsin inhibitor genes to *Rubus* that will stop chewing insects like raspberry beetles and moths in their tracks, and block virus diseases like Arabis mosaic by infecting the virus diseases with a virus.

Today, red raspberries are grown on a commercial scale in Scotland, southern England, eastern Europe and western North America (in the States of Oregon,

Washington, British Columbia). South of the equator they are cultivated in Chile, New Zealand and southern Australia. Black raspberries are farmed in western North America. Raspberries are canned, frozen and made into jams, or used as flavorings for yogurts, ice creams, sweets and liqueurs.

The wineberry, *R. phoenicolasius*, not to be confused with black and red currants that are called wineberries in Scotland—grows wild in northern China and Japan; it was introduced to Western gardens, where it is often grown as an ornamental, in about 1900. Its long, arching canes grow out of a clump, and need to be trained on wires like loganberries. The fruits resemble a blackberry's in shape and size, they are golden, orange, or red.

The cloudberry, *R. chamaemorus*, evolved in the far north. It grows amid the heather and cotton grass of Scandinavia, northern Russia and Canada, and on higher, colder ground in the British Isles. It is one of the very few fruits that can be picked and eaten within the Arctic Circle. A low perennial herb, with erect shoots, creeping rhizomes, white flowers on the ends of its shoots, it produces smallish orange fruits.

The first botanist to describe it was Thomas Penny in the sixteenth century, who found it growing in the Pennines. He sent a drawing and description to Clusius (Charles de l'Écluse), the great Dutch professor of botany at Leiden, who was also director of the Imperial Gardens at Vienna. Gerard illustrated it twice in his 1597 *Herball*. It probably got its name not from clouds that hang around the tops of mountains, but from the old English *clud*, meaning a hill.

Strawberry

Fragaria ananassa of the Rose *family*

Strawberry runners arch over and root at their tips, just like blackberry sprays, which is one of the reasons why the Cambridge botanist, E.J.H. Corner, believed that the flowering plants grew millions of years ago as tall forest trees in the tropics.

He has argued that the trees spread out north and south from the equator, getting smaller and shrubbier and more herbaceous in their colonizing progress. If his theory is correct—and current DNA research seems supportive—then the strawberry is the herbaceous descendant, and the blackberry, with its stout, rather sinister looking new stems covered in prickles and containing a wide pith and searching for somewhere to plant its suckers, is the parental, shrubby link in an evolutionary chain that stretches right back to the first pachycaulous (having a wide pith) forest trees.

So how does the modern pineapple strawberry that we eat with sugar and cream, *Fragaria ananassa*, link onto the end of this chain? Over forty species of strawberry have been identified by botanists in the wild. The commonest, *Fragaria vesca*, grows throughout the northern temperate zones of the world and occurs in North Africa and South America. It is the wild strawberry that we see growing along wood margins and on scrubby land, and particularly where woods have been cleared. The French call it *fraise de bois*. Its name has nothing to do with corn straw; it probably derives from the verb "to strew" and the tangly way it spreads over the woodland floor. It is deliciously juicy or disappointingly dry and seedy, depending on where you pick it. Chalky soil produces the best results. In the seventeenth century, John Aubrey recorded children picking wild strawberries on the limestone around Bath and selling them by the basketful in the city market. But they are always pretty small, as anyone who has tried to pick a worthwhile bowl of wild strawberries for dinner will readily agree.

In Shakespeare's *Richard III*, when Gloucester wants to gain time for his dark designs and get the Bishop of Ely out of the way, he asks him:

When I was last in Holborn,
I saw good strawberries in your
garden there. I do beseech you
send for some of them.

It is of wild strawberries—*vesca*—that Gloucester is thinking.

Small, too, is the Creamy Strawberry, *Fragaria viridis*, with its yellowish fruits that come away with the calyx when you pick them and the musk or Hautbois Strawberry, *Fragaria moschata*, which is a little bigger, but still not big enough. (It was called Hautbois because of its long flower stems rising high above its leaves.) Both species can be picked wild throughout much of Europe and Asia.

The Romans tried to domesticate the wild strawberry, and make it bigger, as early as 200 B.C.; but it stubbornly resisted attempts at enlargement, however good the growing conditions provided. Its earliest mention in English is in a Saxon plant list of the tenth

century. Herbalists record it being grown in medieval European gardens, for ornamental and medicinal reasons as much as for its fresh fruit. Its roots and leaves were, it was believed, astringent—good for diarrhea—and its fresh fruits were employed both as a toothpaste (the juice cleaned up discolored teeth) and a salve for sunburn. Some Alpine varieties of *vesca* and *moschata* were improved in gardens over the years by the French, who still grow them on a minor commercial scale.

Denis Diderot, the French eighteenth-century encyclopaedist and *homme des lettres*, once compared wild strawberries to "the tips of wet-nurses' breasts." But, in Diderot's time, fruit sizes remained disappointingly small. From before the Renaissance to the late eighteenth century, the strawberry was often painted (sometimes hinting at luxury and decadence, the Fall of Man): but there is no huge size increase of fruit over a four-hundred-year period.

L'OFFRANDE DU COEUR *(opposite)*
ARRAS, FIFTEENTH CENTURY
Wool and silk tapestry
Louvre, Paris, France

THE STRAWBERY THIEF, 1883 *(below)*
WILLIAM MORRIS
1834–1896
Textile design
Printed cotton
Private Collection

STUDY OF INSECTS,
BUTTERFLIES AND
FLOWERS
JAN VAN KESSEL, THE
ELDER 1626–1679
Oil on copper
Ashmolean Museum
Oxford, U.K.

Early travelers in America recorded the virgin plains carpeted in bright red strawberries. "They grew so thick that the horses' fetlocks seemed covered in blood," wrote Lewis Mumford. Sadly, such sights are history, the plains are monocultured cornlands now. These were Virginian strawberries, *virginiana*, which the Indians used for bread and drin making and may even have gardened. They still grow in open woodland and hilly ground throughout North America. The early settlers picked them wild and grew them in their gardens, and as early as 1556 were sending seeds back to the Old World, where the first trials seem to have been disappointing. The plants did not often fruit. In the sixteenth century it was not fully appreciated that *virginiana* in the wild is dioecious: you need a male plant simultaneously flowering near to a female plant successfully to achieve pollination and fruiting. Over the next two centuries,

however, garden cultivars were developed from *virginiana* that were both hermaphroditic and self-pollinating. Known as Scarlet strawberries, they were popular for jams and in fresh fruit bowls up until about 1820. They had the lovely red color of modern strawberries, but still lacked the size.

In 1714 a French military engineer and spy called Amédée Frézier was poking around the town of Concepción in Chile. He posed as a tourist and merchant captain, but was in fact engaged in making maps, calculating troop numbers and sketching Spanish military strongpoints for his boss, Louis XIV of France. In a sandy hollow near the town he came upon plants of large-fruited strawberries, which he later described in a book that he wrote about his South American experiences, as "big as a walnut, and sometimes as a hen's egg, of a whitish red, and somewhat less delicious of taste than our wood strawberrie." These were plants of *Fragaria chiloensis*, the Pine or Sand strawberry. It grows wild on the dunes along Chile's coast and inland up into the hills to 5,248ft, and here and there along the Pacific coast of North America from California to the Bering Sea. The Indians had gardened it long before the Spanish arrived and knew all about propagating it from runners. They used it for making dried raisins or wine, or simply ate it fresh. Its fruits were large, firm-fleshed and juicy, and colored red, yellow or white. The Spanish were impressed with it, calling the plant *frutillar* and its fruit *frutilla*, "little fruit," and planted it in Peru and Ecuador, where it is still cultivated in some places.

Frézier potted up some strawberry runners, as he had seen the Indians do, and took them with him on his return voyage to France in 1714. Five plants survived the six month trip to

Marseilles. One was given to the Antoine Jussieu (curator of King's Garden, now the Jardin des Plantes in Paris). The four others were distributed to gardens near Brest, which was Frézier's home ground. They were all female plants, however, and appeared sterile and fruitless. But by 1740, it had begun to dawn on growers that if rows of *chiloensis* were alternated with *virginiana* or *moschata*, adequate fruit set, producing decent-sized berries, could be achieved. The so-called Plougastel strawberry—*chiloensis* cross—pollinated by one of the other two, and named after a village a few miles to the south of Brest—was launched on the Paris and London markets, and sold very well indeed.

Exactly when and where *ananassa*, the Pineapple or Pine strawberry, arose as a vigorous, fertile hybrid between *chiloensis* and *virginiana* is not certain: probably in France and around the middle of the eighteenth century. Some claim that Jussieu had something to do with its invention, others that the French botanist Antoine Duchesne was the first fully to realize and to say in print in 1766, that the new plant was a self-perpetuating hybrid of the two American species. He obtained a plant from London where Phillip Miller, curator of the Chelsea Apothecaries' garden and author of the best-selling *Gardener's Dictionary*, had first described it in 1759. Miller noted it was hermaphroditic, with a large fruit and pineapple taste, but thought it was just a variant of *chiloensis*; he did not notice the *virginiana* characteristics. Miller's plant came from Amsterdam. It had originated in a garden near the city some ten years before.

Ananassa, in fact, may well have come into existence in several European gardens more or

E.D. Smith del.   Weds sculp.

less simultaneously; Duchesne demonstrated—and it has since been repeatedly proved beyond any doubt—that the two American species readily hybridize and produce fertile, vigorous offspring. The good fruit size and flavor of *chiloensis* had combined with the scarlet color of *virginiana*.

Thus the modern strawberry was born, of New World parents, in an Old World birthplace—and was soon embarked on immigrant ships back to the land of its parents, where it thrived.

THE ROSEBERRY STRAWBERRY, 1830
EDWIN DALTON
SMITH, 1800–1866
Engraving
London
Private collection

Apple Malus x domestica *of the* Rose *family*

It seems a shame to pour cold water on the wonderful imagery of the Song of Songs, but the truth is that apples in King Solomon's day, if they were eaten at all in Palestine, were fairly small, bitter and undistinguished: not much consolation for a lover's *tristesse*.

In fact, Solomon was probably thinking of apricots (*Prunus armeniaca*), which are sweet and smell good, and belong to the plum family. The Hebrew word is *tappuach*—like the Latin *malum*, a generic term for fruit. Elsewhere (Proverbs 25:11), a calmer Solomon reflected on the meaning of wisdom: "A word fitly spoken is like apples of gold in pictures of silver." Again, he meant apricots. When William Tyndale, a Gloucestershire man, came to translate the Bible into English from the Hebrew in the sixteenth century, he translated *tappuach* as apples, because he knew apples well in the West Country, and was unfamiliar with apricots.

Apples, the premier fruit crop of the cooler, more temperate regions of the modern world is a fruit that can ripen at higher latitudes than almost any other, except the cloudberry. It originated many millions of years ago in the area between the Black and Caspian seas, just south of the Caucasus mountains; perhaps in the very forests that clothe their southern slopes. The genotype from which all the world's cultivars derive (about two thousand are listed and there must be myriads more that grow, or have grown, in orchards unrecognized) is the Wild or Crab Apple, a low, spreading tree with small, bitter, inedible fruits. It is a self-incompatible species, which means that you need two trees growing near each other to achieve pollination. Once pollinated, though, it grows easily enough from seed: drop a core on fertile ground and in a few years you will have a crab apple tree.

From its central Asian homeland, the Wild Crab spread out in prehistoric times, carried by animals or birds, across the cooler, forested areas of Europe and Asia, and, as it encountered new geographical niches, mutated and speciated to suit. One of the new mutant species was the Domestic Apple, *Malus silvestris* ssp. *domestica*, an upright, spreading tree of very varied size, with a brown-gray, scaly trunk and white, pink-flushed clusters of flowers producing large, round, edible fruits that may be green, yellow or red.

A hundred years ago, apples and pears were lumped together by botanists into a single genus, *Pyrus*; in truth the botanical distinction between the two, which has to do with the separation of their pistil stems (the styles), is technical and fairly slight. Shape is no certain indicator as there are apples that look like pears and pears that look like apples. If in doubt, a rule of thumb for spotting the difference is that pear blossom is nearly always white, rarely pink, and that pears come from, and prefer, more southern latitudes. Apples need nine hundred cold hours to produce

As the apple tree among the trees of the wood, so is my beloved among the sons. I sat down under his shadow with great delight, and his fruit was sweet to my taste. He brought me to the banqueting house, and his banner over me was love. Stay me with flagons, comfort me with apples; for I am sick of love. Song of Solomon II 3–5.

W. Hooker del. 1820.

The Pear-shaped Service

flowers in the spring and on the whole dislike the subtropics and tropics. You can grow apples in Kenya, but only up a mountain.

Today, botanists have separated apples into a separate genus, *Malus*, which contains about thirty wild species. Most have come about as a result of geographical isolation and in Europe and Asia they boil down to three main types: *M. silvestris*, the European crab apple that you can find growing from Tangier to Trondheim, and as far east as the Caspian; the wild apple of central Asia, *M. sieversii*, which Russian botanists like to split up into further local species; and the eastern Siberian and North Chinese crab apple, *M. prunifolia*, 33ft high, with bright red fruits.

The domestic apple did not cross the Gobi desert and enter China from the west until the Middle Ages. Until that date only crab apples were known in the Far East. It is most likely that domestic apples were invented on the western fringes of Asia and that the European and central Asian crab apples, *M. silvestris* and *sieversii*, contributed significant germ plasm.

Crab apples belong to the *Rosaceae*, a very ancient family that includes not only the roses, but disparate plants like plum, raspberry, meadow sweet, and mountain ash. A clue to their aeon-distant past may be glimpsed by the distribution of crab apples in North America. Palaeobotanists—who believe that plants along with humans and animals immigrated into the Americas from Siberia over the frozen Bering Land Bridge—find difficulty in explaining why there are six or more species of crab apple indigenous to the eastern side of the continent, but only one that grows between the Rockies and the Pacific, and why the American and East Asian crabs are so different.

But what if the story is pushed much farther back, to perhaps one hundred million years?

At this time, the angiosperms, the flowering plants, were spreading out from Gondwara, the southern supercontinent (South America, Africa, India, Australia, and the Antarctic) and the northern supercontinent, Laurasia (North America, Europe, Asia, and the Arctic) was splitting up.

Then, the *Persea* genus that includes the avocado, was thought to have hitched a ride on North America when it detached itself from Europe and drifted slowly west across the Atlantic. This was before it became anchored in its present position, some sixty-five million years ago at the end of the Cretaceous period, long before the Bering and Central American Land Bridges respectively froze over or reared up out of the sea. Were the American crab apples shipmates with avocados on that enormous, slow-moving continental raft? Or were they instead immigrants at the dawn of time, from western Europe? It is fun to speculate.

We know that apples were in the second tranche of fruits that were domesticated by man, after olives, grapes, figs, pomegranates, and dates, following the invention of horticulture in the Middle East some 10,000 years ago. They were late-comers because useful apple cultivars can only be "fixed" by clonal grafts—apples grown from seed are wildly unpredictable, and nearly always recessive—and the art of grafting did not arrive in the Mediterranean basin until about the tenth century B.C.

THE PEAR-SHAPED
SERVICE CRAB APPLE
WILLIAM HOOKER
1779–1832
*Natural History Museum
London, U.K.*

However, carbonized remains of small crab apples have been found in Stone Age sites all over Europe from Yugoslavia to Denmark, for instance, in the mud below Swiss lake dwellings. This demonstrates that the European wild apple had extended to its present range by a very early date and formed part of the diet of primitive hunter gathering tribes in northern Europe.

When were apples first domesticated? Small dried apples, cut transversely in half and threaded on strings, have turned up among votive offerings in a Babylonian tomb at Ur, Lower Mesopotamia, dating to the late third millennium B.C. As apples do not grow wild in those hot, southern latitudes between the

Tigris and Euphrates, these stringed apples most probably were cultivated using irrigation and seedlings. Carbonized fruits have also been found at Kadesh-Barne'a oasis, on the border between the Negev and Sinai deserts. The Negev crab apples date to the tenth century B.C. (just the time when King Solomon was singing of apricots) and again were probably grown from seed. Jewish laws strictly forbade plants produced from 'mingled seed', so grafting, even if available, was taboo.

By Greek classical times (sixth century B.C.), the sweet and edible domestic apple had arrived in western Asia and on the Mediterranean's northern shores. Its germ plasm was fixed by clonal grafting techniques learned from the Far East. In his *Odyssey* from the ninth century B.C., Homer described "apple trees with shining fruit" growing in the fabulous orchards of Alkinous, king of Phaeacia (probably the modern Corfu); whether he meant wild or domestic, it is impossible to guess. Five centuries later, Theophrastus, born on the island of Lesbos and successor to Aristotle as principal of the Peripatetic School at Athens, knew all about grafting apples. He described how to bud and graft, and warned against trying to grow apples from cuttings.

Roman writers like Pliny and Columella gave details of highly sophisticated techniques, such as patch budding (cutting a bud off one tree, and patching it onto the branch of another). Pliny listed twenty-three different cultivars of apple, including the Sceptian, named after the freed slave who had discovered it. He particularly liked a small flavorsome apple, the Persian, introduced in the 1st century A.D. from the East. In his fourth *Georgic*, Virgil wrote with great charm,

and some envy, of an old smallholder who cultivated a few poor acres at Tarentum, but lived like a king:

His the first rose of spring, the earliest apples in autumn. When grim winter was splitting the rocks with cold and holding the watercourses with curbs of ice, already that man would be cutting his soft-haired hyacinths, complaining of summer's backwardness and the west winds slow to come.

Virgil did not understand about winter chilling: it was the Tarentum freeze up that would make the old man's apple trees blossom in spring.

Pomona was the Roman goddess of the fruit orchard; both she and Venus, are depicted holding apples or a basket of fruit. The Romans made cider out of apples, as well as eating them fresh or cooked—the emperor Augustus, who rarely touched wine, liked to slake his thirst with a sour apple, fresh or dried. Apple trees were planted by Romans for their shape, blossom, shade and fruit. In town gardens at Pompeii, destroyed by the Vesuvius eruption of A.D. 79, ingenious archaeologists identified various species by making plaster casts of the holes left by charred roots in the volcanic ash. They found root-impressions of almonds, peaches, pomegranates, pears, quinces, cherries and apples.

The eleventh labor of Hercules was bringing home the Golden Apples of the Hesperides out of the mythical West. A fresco in the Villa Poppea at Oplontis, best-preserved of all the Neapolitan villas buried by the seventy-nine A.D. Vesuvian catastrophe, shows Hercules in an orchard of gnarled apple trees. On a rock sit two of the golden apples—or are they pomegranates?

There is evidence that apples were eaten in Roman Britain (pips in Bermondsey mud, seeds in pits at Doncaster and Southwark) but whether they were cultivated is hard to determine. One suspects they were. *Abhall* is Celtic for apple, *avall* is the Cornish word, and the Britons called Glastonbury, Avallon (the Roman name was Avallonia), which suggests that apples were grown there. They were certainly cultivated on the continent in Charlemagne's time and, after the Norman Conquest and rise of the monasteries, references to apple cultivation in Britain come thick and fast. Old English Pearmains were popular for desserts

and cider making in the thirteenth century, and large Costard apples were used for cooking and in pies. A seller of Costard apples off a stall or barrow was called a costermonger.

In Henry VIII's day, the English gene pool was further enriched by cultivars imported from France and Flanders. French Pippin varieties (*pepin* is seedling in French) were

Victorian bourgeoisie, who liked to take their little apple trees with them as they moved from house to house.

The most famous of all English eating apples is Cox's Orange Pippin, which was grown from a pip by a well-to-do Bermondsey brewer called Richard Cox. He retired to Lawn Cottage at Colnbrook and in 1830

THE RIBSTON PIPPIN TREE, 1820

Royal Horticultural Society London, U.K.

prized by the English as dessert apples. Pomatum, a popular cosmetic sold around this time to smooth skin and get rid of freckles, was made of apple pulp, rosewater and pig's fat.

At the end of the sixteenth century, Huguenot refugees from the Low Countries (some of the best market gardeners in Europe at that time) planted orchards in East Anglia and Kent; they close-spaced new varieties using dwarfing techniques hitherto unknown in post-Reformation Britain and invented by medieval monks. In the nineteenth century, nurserymen like Thomas Rivers and John Scott of Merriott developed their own dwarfing rootstocks to suit the mobile

planted up a pot with pips of Ribston Pippin. They originated from pips brought over from Rouen, which were planted in Sir Henry Goodwicke's deer park at Ribston, near Wetherby in Yorkshire in about 1680. The tree was blown down in 1810, but continued to shoot and fruit. Of the seedlings that germinated at Lawn Cottage, one turned out to be Cox's Orange Pippin and another, Cox's Pomona, both are very fine apples indeed.

Bramley's Seedling, most celebrated of all English cooking apples, was grown from a pip at Southwell, Nottinghamshire, in the early 1800s. Its recognition was wonderfully casual, and English. In about 1856, Mr Merryweather, an apprentice nurseryman, saw the vicar's gardener passing with a fine basket of apples. "Where does it grow?" he asked the gardener. "In Mr Bramley's garden, back of his house," came the reply. Merryweather went to look at the tree in full fruit and had not seen the like of it before. He asked for grafts and was told to fetch whatever he wanted from the garden.

The story of the apple's immigration into the U.S. (only crabs existed before Columbus) is as successful as that of any Mellon or Vanderbilt. It sailed the Atlantic with the early colonists and found, on the northeastern seaboard with its cold winters and hot summers, a most suitable environment.

The first apple tree is said to have been planted in America in the early 1600s by John Endicott, governor of Massachusetts. New England's apple blossom in spring was soon a sight to rival that of the native maple leaves in autumn. The Iroquois Indians loved the new fruit. General Sullivan led an expedition against them during the Revolutionary Wars and found orchards groaning with apples.

In the early 1800s, Johnny Appleseed etched his name on American folklore by setting off down the Ohio river with a boatload of apple seeds from the Pennsylvania cider mills. He wore a coffee sack for a shirt, and a saucepan on his head. Preaching the Swedenborgian doctrine, he read from the Bible to whomever would listen and dropped apple seeds wherever he went.

His legend, in fact, is a paradigm for how apples were grown in the early days of the Republic: not so much from grafts, more from seed. Much of this seed might have originated from a hybrid cross between European cultivars, with a dash of native crab. It was a rich gene pool indeed. If the seedlings bore poor fruit, the harvest could always be made into cider, or fed to the homesteaders' pigs and once in a while the fruit turned out to be very good indeed. The Northern Spy, for example, possibly the finest eating apple the continent has ever produced, was a chance seedling found growing in a New York orchard in 1800. Other noteworthy discoveries include the bright red Spitzbergen and Jonathan, both nineteenth-century inventions from New York, or the Rhode Island Greening, grown near Newport by a tavern keeper called Green in the 1700s.

The apple's transfer from the American

Midwest to the Pacific is the stuff of melodrama. In 1845 a nurseryman from Iowa, Henderson Llewelling, set out with his family, and a partner, for the Willamette Valley in Oregon, which he had heard was very fertile. As well as packing seeds, he planted seven hundred varieties of other fruits and grafted apple trees in boxes, all loaded into seven covered wagons.

For the trip across the hot plains beyond the Missouri, he joined a larger wagon train, but his heavily laden plant wagon held up progress, his partner died of cholera, two of his oxen succumbed and his companions implored him to ditch his plants, which, they said, would never cross the mountains. But he refused and his seven wagons were left behind to travel alone. Indians attacked, but, seeing his leafy

cargo waving about in one of the prairie schooners, believed he was protected by spirits, and left him alone. He used up most of his scarce water to feed his plants. Half of them died, but he reached Oregon in October, and floated his family and the remaining plants down the Columbia river to the Willamette Valley, where he arrived in mid-November after a seven-month trek.

By 1853 he was selling apples in San Francisco for a dollar a pound. He grew rich, and moved to California, where he started another nursery and founded the town of Fruitvale, and grew richer still. His story, however, had a sad ending. He grew restless, sold up in California, bought a ship and sailed off to set up a market garden in tropical Honduras, where he went broke.

The heyday of apple varieties in both Europe and America were the years 1790 to 1900. The Victorians grew and ate Pippins and Bramleys, Russets, Swaars, Gravensteins, and Red Astrakhans, to name but a few. Nowadays, ironically, the wonderfully rich gene pool of the apple is being dumbed down for

commercial reasons: apples must refrigerate easily, travel well without bruising, and show a good supermarket color. The Delicious, which originated on a Quaker farm in Iowa in the 1890s and whose shiny red skins took American fruit stalls by storm, keeps forever but tastes like sawdust. The better tasting Golden Delicious (no relation, but named to cash in on the other's popularity) first appeared in West Virginia in the mid-1800s and was probably a cross between an English yellow dessert apple, Golden Reinette, and a Virginian seedling called Grimes Golden.

In 1914, Stark Brothers Nurseries of New York realized what a good commercial apple it was: it kept until spring, fruited early, and cropped heavily in years when other trees were barren. They bought the original hybrid tree for $5,000 and set to work to publicize the new fruit. Now Golden Delicious is grown all over the world, from France to South Africa, from Mexico to Tasmania, to the miserable exclusion of older, wiser, more subtle varieties which are gradually becoming extinct.

Pear

Pyrus communis *of the* Rose *family*

Wild pears, from which all our cultivated pears descend, originated long before historic time somewhere in central Asia, probably, like apples and grapes, in the region of the Caucasus mountains between the Black and Caspian seas.

Pears belong to the *Rosaceae*, a very ancient family which includes disparate plants like brambles, meadow sweet and mountain ash. The family goes back one hundred million years, to the time when the flowering plants were setting out from the primeval equatorial jungle to colonize the rest of the planet and long before our continents drifted into their present positions on the global map. *Homo habilis*, our apeman, crude, tool-using ancestor, emerged from Africa into the Levant about two million years ago. Plants like the *Rosaceae* put us in our historical place.

A hundred years ago, apples and pears were lumped together by botanists into a single genus, *Pyrus*. Today, apples are given separate status. The botanical difference between the two is slight, and has to do with the separation of their pistil stems (the styles). Shape is an uncertain indicator: there are apples that look like pears and vice versa. A rough way of telling them apart is that pear blossom is usually white, not flushed with pink, and that pears prefer sunnier, more southern latitudes and require less winter chilling to make good blossom in spring.

From their central Asian homeland wild pears spread out into most of temperate Europe and Asia. As they encountered new

geographical niches, they mutated and speciated to suit. They were, and are, self-incompatible, which means that you need two genetically different pear trees growing near each other to achieve cross pollination and fruit set. Once pollinated, though, the seeds grow well: drop a core on fertile ground and in a few years a pear seedling may grow.

Today, about thirty different wild *Pyrus* species have been identified, from the Atlantic coast of Spain east to the China seas. There were no pears in the Americas before Columbus. Most are rather thorny trees with small, hard, gritty, more or less inedible fruits; their cores are surrounded by a great number of stone cells, which makes eating them a less than pleasant experience. They are taller and

SMALL BIRD WITH PEARS
ALEXANDRA WALKER
Fresco technique based on original, A.D. *60*
Villa Poppea
Oplontis, Italy

MADONNA AND CHILD

ALBRECHT DURER

1471–1528

Galleria degli Uffizi

Florence, Italy

more columnar than apples. The biggest grow up to 66ft high and the timber is very dense and is prized by cabinet makers.

Wild species readily interbreed with cultivars. Growing on the edges of orchards, they are what the Germans call *werwildert*: naturalized in the wild. From time immemorial, peasant farmers have grafted scions of cultivars on to wild stocks growing in a hedge or wood. So sorting out the antecedents of the cultivated pear is more of an art than a science.

The European cultivated pear descends from a group of wild pears (collectively known as *P. pyraster* and *caucasica*) that grow in Europe, Asia Minor, and the Caucasus; while Asian pears, which are round, juicy, less flavorsome and slightly gritty (also known as "sand pears," they look like russet apples) descend from species such as *pyrifolia* and *ussuriensis*, which grows in the Far East.

Stone Age hunter gatherers in Europe ate

wild pears long before they were domesticated. Small carbonized fruits, sometimes cut in half and probably dried for winter consumption, have turned up in neolithic sites (*c.*4,000 B.C.) in Germany, Switzerland, northern Italy and Greece.

The earliest known literary reference occurs on a Sumerian clay tablet, *c.*2,750 B.C., from southern Iraq, which recommends making a medical poultice by mixing beer and oil with pulverized thyme, pears and figs—these may well have been cultivated pears. There is some evidence that apples were being grown in Mesopotamian orchards around this time—and pears are much more comfortable in southern heat.

In the Tomb of Nakht (*c.*1,400 B.C.) in Egypt's Valley of the Kings at Western Thebes, there is a lovely wall painting of two women sitting behind a blind harpist and holding fruit that look uncommonly like large, cultivated pears.

Pears, like apples, were in the late, second tranche of fruits to be domesticated in the Near East, long after figs, grapes, dates, olives, and pomegranates. Their culture probably arrived in the Aegean basin from the Fertile Crescent around Homer's time, 1,000 B.C., when the technique of grafting was beginning to be understood. Pears live longer than apples— some trees last three hundred years—but the only certain way of perpetuating good, edible genotypes is by clonal grafts. Pears grown from seed are recessive and usually worthless.

Homer mentions pears in the *Odyssey*— Laertes, Odysseus's father, is found digging under a pear tree, but whether it is wild or cultivated is anybody's guess. Laertes is described as being in his garden, so perhaps a

Pyrus communis

cultivar is implied. Theophrastus (*c.* 300 B.C.), guardian of Aristotle's children and his successor as head of the Peripatetic School at Athens, certainly knew the difference between wild and cultivated pears: he described three cultivars and stressed that they needed to be grown from grafts, not seed.

A century later, Cato, that stiff Roman republican of the old school, knew of six. By Pliny's time (first century A.D.) the list had swelled to thirty-five. He liked the Crustumian pears best, which grew in Latium near the Tiber, and juicy Falernians from about thirty miles north of Rome (good, he said, for making perry), and dark pears from Syria.

The Romans were very keen gardeners who planted and collected from all over their empire. Research at Fishbourne palace in West Sussex indicates that they may have introduced the cultivated pear to Britain. The wild pear was already there: in later, Anglo-Saxon charters it is one of the six most common trees to be cited as boundary landmarks, either freestanding or in hedgerows, and it occurs frequently in place names.

In Italy, the Romans liked to grow pears in their villa gardens, often planted in formal quincunx patterns (four at each corner, one in the middle) and flanking a central marble watercourse. At Pompeii, archaeologists have identified pear root impressions in the layers of volcanic ash. A fresco in the House of the Fruit Orchard illustrates, among other fruits, what looks like a pear tree. Another, in the House of the Marine Venus, features a pear with a dove-like bird sitting in its branches.

A list of plants required by Charlemagne to be grown in France in the ninth century included eating, cooking, and winter-keeping pears and,

after the Dark Ages, the spread of the monastic movement throughout Europe ensured that knowledge of pear culture was not forgotten.

The Wardon or Warden, a large cooking pear used in pies and pastries throughout the Middle Ages, is claimed to have been first pear

STILL LIFE WITH FRUIT, 1888
PAUL GAUGUIN
1848–1903
Oil on canvas
Pushkin Museum
Moscow, Russia

THE CHAUMONTELLE PEAR (opposite)
WILLIAM HOOKER
1779–1832
Natural History Museum
London, U.K.

to be grown by Cistercian monks of Wardon in Bedfordshire in the fourteenth century; it may in fact date back to Roman times.

In 1495, Charles VIII, after his conquest of the Kingdom of Naples, imported into France the very same pear that Pliny had put top of his list, called the Crustumian from near the river Tiber, in central Italy. It was, and still is, a very fine cooking pear.

In 1770, a schoolmaster at Aldermaston in Berkshire grew an improved mutant, called Williams' Bon Chrétien, also still widely grown today. The new variety was taken to Massachusetts in America whence, in 1797,

under the name of Bartlett (its original name having been forgotten), the descendant of Pliny's Roman pear traveled west and became a mainstay of the Californian canning industry. Its overland, northern route into California was in fact more typical of apples from New England.

Pears are a Spanish fruit. They enjoy the hot Spanish sun. They sailed with missionary padres and colonists to Mexico and the Spanish Main, then moved north up the Pacific coast in the eighteenth century. You can still see ancient specimens of pear growing in old Franciscan and Dominican mission gardens in California.

Pyrus communis

Doyenné de Comice, one of the finest dessert pears, was raised from seed by the Horticultural Society of Maine et Loire at Angers in France. It first fruited in 1849 and was brought to England nine years later.

Conference, one of the most popular modern commercial pears, was introduced by an English nursery, Rivers of Sawbridgeworth, at the end of the nineteenth century.

Perry pears probably arose from hybrids of *Pyrus communis* and *Pyrus nivalis*, a native of southern Europe with white downy undersides to its leaves. They are the pear equivalent of cider apples and have been crushed and pressed for fermentation since Roman times. In the early 1700s, the heyday of perry production in England, they were grown on the heavier clay soils, which apples disliked, of Gloucestershire, Worcestershire and Herefordshire. Remnants of the perry orchards remain today, tall trees with white canopies of blossom in the spring. In a good year a mature tree can yield a ton of pears.

During the Napoleonic wars, when wine imports were restricted, perry farmers cashed in with their fizzing champagne taste alike. In the nineteenth century, though, they lost out to factory-made beer—the English climate could not guarantee the hot, sunny summers the trees required. But as late as the First World War, the Blakeney Red variety from Gloucestershire made perry and was stewed and put into cans for the troops. A local boast was that it had "won that thur war—it gave Tommy good drink, good food, and clothes for his back." Today, in many a West Midlands farmyard the heavy stone mills and huge presses lie broken and abandoned, overgrown with nettles or sold to decorate pubs.

The Chaumontelle Pear

Almond, apricot, cherry, peach, & plum

Prunus *genus of the* Rose *family*

The ancestor of the *Prunus* genus originated long before historic time, somewhere in the mountain valleys and upland forests of central Asia. Since then it has evolved into over one hundred wild species of deciduous trees and shrubs and colonized the northern temperate regions of the world: from Asia east to China, Japan and north America, and west to Europe.

FRESCO OF A
PARTRIDGE EATING
CHERRIES
*Villa Poppaea,
Oplontis, Italy*

The important fruit-bearing species of the genus—almond, apricot, cherry, peach, and plum—still remember their high-country origin: to achieve fruit set they demand winter chilling, plenty of summer sunshine and they detest the tropics.

The sweet cherry or Gean (*Prunus avium*) evolved at a fairly early stage from the ancestral protoparent. It is a large tree, growing up to 82.5ft high with dark, shiny bark, a round outline, white flowers and bittersweet, round and reddish-black berries. Over the millennia it

migrated west from its center of origin and is now a wild native of Europe, North Africa, Turkey and the lands either side of the Caucasus. Primitive man gathered it: cherry stones from wild fruits have been found at Neolithic and Bronze Age (5,000–1,500 B.C.) sites as far apart as Turkey, Italy, Portugal, and central Europe.

The cherry was brought into cultivation rather late, in the Greece/Asia Minor area in the middle of the first millennium B.C. This was many centuries after the "first wave" of domestication of grapevine, olive, fig, date and pomegranate, all of which are easy to multiply by cuttings or transplants. *P.avium* is more difficult to grow; it is unable to pollinate itself, so you have to plant several trees in a stand to achieve cross pollination and fruit set. More crucially, its propagation, like that of apples, pears and plums, is best achieved not by seed or cuttings, but by grafting—and grafting, invented in China, was unknown in Europe at least until Classical times.

The Greeks and Romans were both familiar

with the technique of growing cherries. Theophrastus (372–287 B.C.), a pupil of Plato and guardian of Aristotle's children, mentions its cultivation in his *History of Plants*. Pliny writes that in the 60s B.C. the Roman general Lucullus brought a superior cherry variety to Rome from Asia Minor, giving it pride of place among his spoils of the Mithridatic Wars. A delightful Roman wall painting of a bird eating cherries at the Villa Poppaea at Oplontis, confirms the Roman interest in cherries. It was found in the shadow of Vesuvius and was buried by the mountains' eruption in A.D. 79.

The sour or Morello cherry (*Prunus cerasus*) is a cross between *avium* and the Ground cherry, *P. fruticosa*, a shrub with small, very bitter, unpalatable fruits that grows wild in central and eastern Europe and northeast Turkey. The result, the sour cherry, is more shrub than tree and rarely higher than 26ft. Unlike *avium*, it is able to pollinate itself. Its range in the wild is much the same as the sweet cherry and it is cultivated for its small, sour red fruits, good for jams and liqueurs. *Fruticosa's* center of origin is central and western Asia, so it is probable that the cross occurred very early, before both species moved west and long before *avium* was domesticated on the rim of Europe.

As the Roman empire declined, so did the culture of cherries, and it did not revive again until about the sixteenth century, when sweet

STILL LIFE OF CHERRIES AND PEACHES

BALTHASAR VAN DER AST *c.* 1593–1657
Johnny van Haeften Gallery, London, U.K.

Prunus

Asian birthplace via China, where they dropped off another species *P. tomentosa*, then via Siberia and the Bering Land Bridge, before it became the Bering Sea. In America, the European sour cherries found that the east coast suited them. The sweet cherries pushed on farther west.

The almond (*Prunus communis*) is a close relative of the peach *(Prunus persica)* and has similar fruits, but they are generally smaller, ovoid, and flattened. The ancestral species of *Prunus,* from which both forms derive, split in central Asia and one half moved southwest evolving into the almond, while the other half moved east to China and became the peach.

Wild almonds like dry, Mediterranean, *maquis* conditions and thrive on rocky south-facing hillsides in Northern Africa and the Levant, or the arid Steppes of Caucasia, north-east Turkey and Afghanistan. They are small trees up to 20ft high —double that in cultivation—with black bark and large, pink flowers, appearing from January to March before the leaves.

It is a wonder that they were ever brought into cultivation for most wild types have, as a chemical defense, intensely bitter seeds in the nuts. When mixed with water they produce prussic acid, a deadly, fast-acting poison. A mouthful of masticated seeds will kill a man, but heating renders them harmless: oil of bitter almonds, extracted from the seed, is used to make cakes, sweets, and marzipan.

The world's premier nut crop today, almonds were unlikely candidates for cultivation as they were poisonous and unable to self pollinate or be

and sour cherries were grown once more in Europe, especially in Germany. They sailed westwards with the early settlers to America— and met their relatives, the American wild sand cherries, *P. besseyi* and *pumila.* These varieties beat them to the New World by millennia, having traveled the other way from their central

CHERRY TREE FROM
DE STIRPIUM
HISTORIA (*opposite*)

FIFTEENTH CENTURY

Lindley Library
Royal Horticultural
Society, London, U.K.

GEORGE
WASHINGTON,
1732–1799

Illustration
Private Collection

propagated by suckers or cuttings. Nevertheless, they were domesticated very early, not later than the third millennium B.C.

The earliest evidence of wild almonds being gathered and eaten comes from Stone Age (c.8,000 B.C.) caves in southern Greece, and shells of what are believed to be cultivated almonds have been identified at the early Bronze Age (2,800 B.C.) site of Bab edh-Dhra in Jordan's Dead Sea Basin, as well as at other similar sites in the near East, Greece, and Egypt. Dried out fruits were found in Tutankhamun's tomb (c.1,325 B.C.) and by classical times the almond crop was established.

The path to cultivation seems to have happened like this: mutants lacking the bitter poison—nowadays cultivated as the sweet almond, *P. dulcis*—were selected and and multiplied from seed, 2,000 years before the art of grafting became known in the Mediterranean world. Almond seedlings show a wide variation but if the parents are sweet almonds, approximately seventy-five percent of the seedlings will be sweet and the bitter almonds can be weeded out. It is a hit or miss cultural technique that is still practiced today.

In the Middle Ages, almonds were imported into northern Europe by the wagonload; meat and almond stews were standard fare. Salted almonds, nibbled throughout dinner, were believed to prevent drunkenness. An inventory of the effects of the Queen of France from 1372 lists only twenty pounds of sugar, but five hundred pounds of almonds.

Today, in the Levant and India they are still used to flavor meat dishes, but in the West they are mostly used by bakers in flaked, powdered or paste form to make confectionery like nougat, or are eaten as dessert fruits. Today, they thrive anywhere with a frost-free Mediterranean climate that grows chilly in winter: in California, South Africa and Australia, as well as Spain, Italy and Provence.

The peach (*Prunus persica*), the other half of the central Asian, West-East ancestral split with the almond, almost certainly evolved in China. Wild peaches occur in the Tibetan highlands and western China and there is literary evidence that peaches were under cultivation there around 2,000 B.C., long before they had ever been heard of in Europe.

They arrived in Greece from Persia during the fourth century B.C., probably as a result of Alexander the Great's Asian campaigns as far as the Indus. Lucullus, another general made fabulously rich from his campaigns in Asia Minor (in about 60 B.C.), brought back peaches from Pontus on the south shore of the Black Sea and planted them in the new gardens he designed in the middle of Rome, where the church of Trinità dei Monti now stands, at the top of the Spanish Steps. By the time Vesuvius erupted in A.D. 79, affluent Pompeians were cultivating peaches in the courtyards of their town villas for shade, scent, flowers and fruit.

The peach was welcomed with delight by the Romans, who named it the Persian apple, and by the end of the first century they were growing it in most provinces of the empire.

Today it is grown in open orchards as far north as the Loire and southern Germany. In Britain, the peach was established at the beginning of the sixteenth century after knowledge of its culture in Europe had all but died during the Dark Ages. In China, the land of its birth, its appreciation never seems to have faltered: Marco Polo saw yellow and white peaches, "great delicacies," for sale in the 1290s in Kinsai (Hang-chau) and, in another province, giant fruits "weighing fully two small pounds apiece." After the voyages of discovery, it travelled west from Europe to the New World and crossed the equator to South Africa and Australia. Both are now major producers of peaches, though much of the crop ends up canned as the fruit does not stay fresh for long.

The apricot (*Prunus armeniaca*) grows wild in the Tien Shan mountains of central Asia in eastern Tibet, and in northern China. Its wild fruits are small and poor-tasting, with bitter nuts. Whether and precisely when it was first improved by cultivation in central Asia or China is unknown—most likely in China, like

SINO-TIBETAN ALTAR CLOTH

SIXTEENTH CENTURY
Silk, gold thread
Spink & Son, London, U.K.
The goddess offers peaches to the buddhas of meditation

armeniaca after its place of origin. Its characteristic, large stones have been found at Roman sites all over the empire. Today, the U.S. is the leading producer of apricots, fresh and canned; in Europe, the main growing countries are Hungary, Spain, France and Italy. Apricots are rich in vitamin A and proteins, and are good for flavoring ice cream and yogurts, and filling cakes and tarts. In central Asia, they are still dried and stored for the winter.

The plum's origins are the most complicated of all the *Prunus* fruits. There are five main types of cultivated plum and five supposed areas of origin: *P. domestica* (Old World plum, from Europe); *P. insititia* (damson, greengages and bullaces, from western Asia); *P. cerasifera* (Myrobalan or Cherry plum, from central and west Asia); *P. salicina* (the early-flowering Japanese plum that grows wild in China) and *P. americana* (from North America). If only things were that simple!

It was long assumed, for instance, that the European plum, *domestica*, and the damson and bullace, *insititia*, evolved from a cross in Europe between the wild, bitter sloe, *spinosa*, which grows throughout the cooler parts of Europe and western Asia, and the Myrobalan's wild form, *divaricata*, a spiny, shrubby tree that ranges from the Balkans through Caucasia to southwest Asia and reproduces from seed. But some botanists now suspect that the sloe had nothing at all to do with the plum's evolution; the bridging link from the cherries (and thence from the *Prunus* protoparent) may well be an early form of the wild Myrobalan in central Asia, which evolved westwards into the damson and European plum and eastwards to make the Japanese and American species.

THE ROYALE PLUM

WILLIAM HOOKER

1779–1832

Natural History Museum
London, U.K.

the peach. It is a sturdy, frost-hardy tree, growing up to 33ft high in cultivation, with white or pale, pink flowers. Its orange-yellow fruits are smaller than the peach and the drier flesh peels away easily from the stone. It arrived in the Levant along the Silk Road from Armenia or Iran in about the first century B.C. The Romans thought it was a species of plum—it does share the same sub-genus *Prunophora*—and they called it

Such a theory parallels the almond peach West-East split.

In truth, we know as little about the domestication of the plum as we do about its early evolution. Plum stones believed to be from wild species (*divaricata* and *insititia*) have been found at Neolithic and Bronze Age sites in Switzerland, Italy, Germany and Austria. They were probably gathered or anyway picked off wild trees allowed to grow near the settlements. Stones from domestic plums were unearthed from late Iron Age levels at Maiden Castle in Dorset, which suggests that though not a native fruit, *P. domestica* was growing in Britain before the Romans arrived.

The Greeks and Romans of the pre-Christian era do not seem to have been very familiar with plums. Writers that developed rural themes like Homer and Hesiod ignore them. Theophrastus mentions them only once *en passant*; Cato the Censor (second century B.C.) and Varro (first century B.C.) are silent. But by Pliny's time (first century A.D.), plums were commonplace in Roman orchards and his contemporary Columella, who farmed near Cádiz in Spain, wrote of the fruit harvest:

. . . and the panniers are piled high with apricots and plums and damsons too and fruits once sent by Persis barbarous.

During the Dark Ages in Europe the domestic plum probably survived more or less in the wildwood and hedgerows. Its stones have been discovered at Viking levels from archaeological digs at York. It features in a ninth-century list of fruits that Charlemagne enjoyed. A tenth-century Anglo-Saxon herbal also makes it clear that plums were beginning to make a comeback in English orchards. The plum would have been brought back into cultivation by Cistercian and Benedictine monks—in 1270 the monk responsible for Westminster Abbey's gardens was required to supply the monastery with plums and cherries, as well other fruits.

But plums in medieval times were mostly cooked—fresh fruit was connected with summer heat and dysentery, even with the ague (malaria), a killer at that time, even in England. A fifteenth-century English schoolboy complained, "I ate damsons yesterday, which made my stomach so raw that I could eat no manner of flesh." "Raw pears a poison," went the proverb, "baked a medicine be."

The Mary Rose, flagship of Henry VIII that was sunk in 1545 and raised in 1982, carried over one hundred plums of five varieties: bullace; red cherry plum (Myrobalan); yellow cherry plum (Myrobalan variety); Catalonia (it still exists and is one of the earliest plums); and Reine Claude (greengage).

The greengage acquired its English name by accident. It came from Armenia via Greece and Italy to France, where it was named Reine Claude after the wife of Francois I (1494–1547). Early in the eighteenth century a Roman Catholic priest sent it from Paris to his brother, Sir Thomas Gage, who lived at Hengrave Hall near Bury St Edmunds. The French label went missing in the way that labels do and Gage's gardener called it greengage. The name stuck. In 1731, Phillip Miller, head of the Apothecaries' Garden at Chelsea, pronounced Greengage the finest plum in England.

Blackcurrants, redcurrants, whitecurrants, & gooseberries

Ribes genus of the Currant *family*

You would be forgiven for thinking that the cultivation of currants is very old. In a sense, it is—but not the red and blackcurrants that we grow in our fruit cages today. In fact, it is the dried, seedless fruits of the small Zante currant grape that have been eaten and exported since before the Renaissance, and probably since Classical times.

A cultivar of *Vitis vinifera* that likes the richer, better-irrigated valley soils of southwestern Greece and the Ionian islands, currant-grapes were known as *raisins de Corauntz* in the thirteenth century. Corinth was the main port of exit: hence their name and because they look like dried blackcurrants, the confusion.

Red and blackcurrants have probably only been cultivated for the last four or five hundred years. They are never mentioned by Classical writers, and the first known published description of a redcurrant (*Ribes rubrum*) is in a German manuscript of the early fifteenth century.

The fruit was first illustrated in the *Mainz Herbarius* of 1484; its oldest mention in English is in Turner's 1548 *Names of Herbes.* For a Tudor herbalist like William Turner the interest of the plant was probably not so much as a food, eaten fresh or cooked for jellies and jams, but more for its medicinal qualities. The juice was considered good for fevers and a useful treatment for the loosening of the bowels.

Over 150 species of *Ribes* shrubs have been identified by botanists growing in the wild, throughout the colder, temperate regions of Europe, Asia and North America, and in the South American Andes as far south as Patagonia. Three have been involved in the evolution of the cultivated redcurrant: *R. rubrum*, the northern redcurrant, which grows in northern and central Europe and northern Asia; *R. sativum*, a larger-fruited species with purple-green flowers that grows in western Europe and is responsible for both red- and white-fruited cultivars; and *R. petraeum*, an upright shrub which grows in the mountains of western Europe and North Africa, and in Siberia; its flowers are red or pink, its leaves roundish and the fruits red to nearly black and acidic.

All three are hardy perennial shrubs, and easily grown from clonal cuttings. The first to be domesticated was probably *sativum*, in the area of northwestern Europe around Holland

and Germany. Leonard Fuchs or "Fuchsius," professor of medicine at Tubingen University on the banks of the Neckar in Germany, published in 1542 his *De Historia Stirpium*, one of the first herbals to illustrate plants with some degree of botanical accuracy. He included a drawing of what looks like *sativum* in his book.

In 1561, Conrad Gesner, a German-Swiss naturalist, who was a friend and correspondent of William Turner, dug up *petraeum* growing wild in the woods near Berne and planted it in his garden. Its fruits were large and juicy.

In the late sixteenth century, *sativum* and *petraeum* travelled from the Continent to Britain, where the eating, jamming and jelly-making potential of cultivated redcurrants was becoming more widely appreciated (although herbalists were still recommending redcurrant syrup as a febrifuge and aperient).

Redcurrants in a Basket

Boris Lavrenko
b. 1920
Oil on canvas
Roy Miles Fine Paintings
London, U.K.

A popular way of growing currants at this time was not in, but round, a garden, enclosing vegetables or herbs as a hedging plant. Small-berried *rubrum* was brought into cultivation, too, around this time. You can still see it growing wild in ancient deciduous woodland in southern England, especially along river banks among alders and willows. It is recognizable by its greenish-brown flowers and small, pale, red to almost white, translucent berries.

Perhaps Turner had *rubrum* in mind when he wrote in the 1568 edition of his herbal:

Ribes is a little bushe and hath leves lyke a vyne and in the tops of the bushe are red berries in clusters in taste at the first somethinge sower but pleasant enough when they are fully ripe. I have seene them growinge in gardens in Englande and also by a water side at Clower in Somersetshyre in the possession of Maister Horner.

The Americas have no native redcurrant species. European cultivars sailed across the Atlantic with the early colonists, probably in the seventeenth century, and thrived in the New World. At the end of the nineteenth century, however, white pine blister rust (*Cronartium ribicola*) was imported with pine seedlings from Europe, and the culture of currants (both red and blackcurrants can host the disease) is now banned in large areas of the American continent, where five-needled pines are grown as a forest crop.

Red and whitecurrant varieties, unlike raspberries, are very long-lived: the two main cultivars, Red and White Dutch, that were recommended by English garden catalogs of the late 1700s, are still grown today. In 1826, the Horticultural Society (it became Royal in 1861) grew thirteen varieties, nine red and four white, in its collection at Chiswick; all more or less derived from Red and White Dutch.

By the end of the nineteenth century the number of varieties available to growers had more than trebled. Houghton Castle (*rubrum* x *sativum*) was introduced in about 1820, and Raby Castle, another *rubrum* derivative, in about 1860, both from gardens in the north of England.

Under cultivation, *sativum* evolved several early ripening, large-fruited varieties, including Cherry. Its unusually large berries were spotted by a French gardener in 1843 in a batch of plants imported from Italy and it quickly became a favorite cultivar in northern Europe and America. Other *sativum* derivatives were Versailles, discovered in 1835; Fay's Prolific, bred in Portland, New York, in about 1868; and Red Lake, invented by the Minnesota Fruit Breeding Farm in 1920. Meanwhile *Petraeum* gave rise to varieties like Gondouin (*petraeum* x *sativum*), Prince Albert (known in Germany in the early eighteenth century) and Seedless Red.

The leaves and fruit of the blackcurrant (*R. nigrum*) smell strongly of tomcats and this may be the reason why it makes a belated, rather shamefaced appearance in English herbals,

nearly one hundred years after the redcurrant. It was ignored by classical writers and neither Turner, in his *Names of Herbes* (1548), nor Gerard in the first edition of his *Herball* (1597) gave it a mention. The first published reference to it in English is in John Parkinson's *Paradisus* (1629). He was not particularly encouraging:

The black Curran bush riseth higher than the white-black berries of the bigness of the smaller red Currans — both branches, leaves and fruit have a kind of stinking sent with them, yet they are not unwholesome but the berries are eaten of many, without offending either taste or smell. Some use both the leaves and berries in sauces and other meates, and are well pleased both with the savour and taste although many mislike it.

The blackcurrant had probably been gathered in the wild long before Parkinson put pen to paper, particularly in Russia, where its juice was made into wine (sometimes fermented with honey) and medicinal drinks. The earliest garden cultivars are very likely to have been Russian.

Nigrum ranges in the wild from northern Europe to northern and central Asia as far as

GOOSEBERRIES, CHERRIES AND REDCURRANTS
JOHANN JAKOB
c.1600–1679
Bibliothèque Nationale Paris, France

PRESERVING JAM

FREDERICK DANIEL
HARDY
1826–1911
*Bourne Gallery, Reigate
Surrey, U.K.*

the Himalayas. It is a hardy shrub, up to 6.6ft high, with stout branches, dull white flowers and smallish fruit; from this species nearly all our cultivars have derived. Farther east, in Manchuria and Korea, grows *R. ussuriense*, which is like *nigrum* but suckering, and in eastern Siberia there is a very winter-hardy species called *dikushka*. *Ussuriense* has been crossed with *nigrum* by twentieth-century breeders in Canada to combat the white pine blister rust that north American foresters fear so much, and *dikushka* has lent resistance to

diseases like mildew and leaf spot. Two native American species have been used by breeders, too: *bracteosum* and *petiolare*. *Bracteosum*, the Californian blackcurrant, which grows as far north as Alaska, has large, maple-like leaves and long fruit clusters. It stands erect, about 10ft high; *petiolare*, half its size, ranges from British Columbia to Montana, and south to Oregon and Utah.

Is *nigrum* native to Britain or a garden escape? Probably the former. A good place to see it growing wild is in the East Anglian Fens. Its first recorded planting in an English garden was at Hatfield House in 1611, when John Tradescant imported twelve plants from Holland for the Earl of Salisbury and presented his bill: "for on dussin of great blacke currants 1s[hilling]."

More than 150 years elapsed, though, before the English began taking blackcurrants to their hearts as garden fruits. Seventeenth-century herbalists and garden writers were, on the whole, dismissive: as late as 1779 John Abercrombie in *The British Fruit Gardener* recommended growing the odd bush in one's garden, but mainly for medicinal reasons. At this time, country people were in the habit of using the wild fruits to make hot drinks or "robs" for sore throats—still soothed today by blackcurrant pastilles.

By 1800, blackcurrant culture was becoming more widespread in both Europe and America. Popular varieties were Baldwin, Black Naples and Black Grape, all of unknown origin but still in existence. In the nineteenth century, American growers relied mainly on cultivars imported from Europe or Canada—several new ones, such as Goliath, Carter's Champion (a chance seedling found in an Essex garden in 1880) and Boskoop Giant from Holland, were developed about this time. When white pine blister rust arrived in the late 1800s, the culture of blackcurrants in America never fully recovered.

Today, Russia, Britain, Germany, and Poland are the world's leading producers. The crop is used to make jams and a concentrated syrup drink for children, high in vitamin C, and to flavor yogurts and ice cream. In France, it provides the base for the liqueur, Cassis.

The bristles on the fruit of the wild gooseberry (*Ribes grossularia*), like the thorns

on the thorn apple, have been cited as evidence of great antiquity: something very like gooseberries, botanists believe, grew in the world's first, primeval forests.

Whatever its age and origin though, this smallish (3.3ft-high), spiny, deciduous shrub, which grows wild in many parts of Europe, North Africa, and the Caucasus, is the source of all the gooseberries that we grow in our gardens. In the British Isles (where it may well be a garden escape) you can find it in scrubby, deciduous woodland, and in niches of stone walls or hedgerows; it has greenish flowers and its tart, dryish fruits, which can be red, yellow or green, are usually ripe enough, for cooking anyway, by the middle of July.

Like red and blackcurrants, gooseberries were first domesticated fairly late, sometime during the Middle Ages, and probably in Continental Europe. There is a record of gooseberry bushes, costing three pence each, being imported from France in 1275 for planting in Edward I's garden at the Tower of London. Then silence reigns for over two hundred years, with England in the grip of civil wars, famine, and disease, until 1509, the year that Henry VIII became king. Better times brought about a gardening renaissance and "pale" Flemish gooseberry plants were imported from the Continent.

William Turner wrote in 1548, in his *Names of Herbes*, that he had seen gooseberries growing only in gardens in England, and wild in the German countryside (which supports the notion that they are an English garden escape). Later in the sixteenth century, writers like Thomas Hill and Heresbachius were recommending planting gooseberry suckers as garden hedging plants, or for sprawling over arbors. Heresbachius referred to the gooseberry in 1578 as:

a common bushe....it will easily growe, but that is something troublesome, by reason of his sharpe prickles to be bend about sommer houses.

By the end of the century, its culture in England had become fairly widespread, with a number of varieties from which to choose. John Gerard illustrated a gooseberry (it was called "feaberry" in his native Cheshire) in his 1597 herbal, and wrote:

There be divers sorte of the Gooseberries, some greater, others lesse, some rounde, others long and some of red colour....These plants do grow in London gardens and else where in great abundance. This shrub had no name among old writers, who as we deeme knew it not or else esteemed it not.

How did it get its name? One theory is that it had to do with a medieval cooking sauce, a mixture of gooseberries, sugar, and fennel, which accompanied young geese; another that it derived, via the north country "grozer" or "grozzle," from the French word for redcurrant, *groseille*. In France, the gooseberry was, and still is, used in a sauce for mackerel: hence its name *groseille à maquereau*. The origins of its other English name, feaberry, however, are a mystery.

Gooseberries originated on the European Continent, but it was the English who took them to their hearts, improving them in their gardens and raising new varieties from seed. They used them for tarts, sauces, pies, and chutneys, put the young leaves into salads, preserved the berries in bottles for the winter, fermented them to make a light, sparkling wine, distilled them to make an acceptable brandy, ate the yellow varieties for desserts, used them as a substitute for unripe grapes or crab apples in verjuice (a sort of vinegar), or heated their juice in hot broths for the ague.

In the 1740s, Lancashire handloom weavers began competing against each other over who could grow the biggest gooseberry. It became a craze throughout the north. Gooseberry clubs were formed, registers maintained, seeds painstakingly selected, cultural secrets jealously guarded. The *Gooseberry Grower's Register*, published annually in Manchester from 1786, gave details of winning weights. It proved valuable source material for Charles Darwin when he wrote *The Variation of Plants and Animals under Domestication* in the 1860s. Gooseberry fruits in the wild, he found, averaged ¼oz. In 1786, a winning weight was about ½oz.

The variety London, first grown in Norwich in 1831, beat off all comers for thirty-six seasons and weighed in at a colossal 2oz in 1852. By the end of the nineteenth century there were nearly one thousand varieties available, mainly due to the stimulus of the gooseberry clubs.

Today, Britain is still the premier growing area for gooseberries. Mostly they are grown in gardens, but some are cultivated on commercial farms as an intercrop between fruit trees. The plants require cool growing conditions in the summer, so they are rarely seen in southern Europe. Fruits are used fresh, bottled, canned, jammed or in tarts.

The worcesterberry (*Ribes divaricatum*), once thought to be an English, nineteenth-century cross between a gooseberry and blackcurrant (the two can hybridize, but their offspring is sterile), is in fact an American West coast native. It has smaller fruits than the gooseberry, about 0.4in across, black or dark purple, and grows along the Rocky Mountains from British Columbia down to California.

GOOSEBERRIES ON A BRANCH
Postcard

Mulberries

Morus nigra, alba *and* rubra *of the* Mulberry *family*

Black mulberries from the Caucasus for fruits, leaves of white mulberries from the Chinese mountains for feeding silkworms—the two species have been endlessly confused over the centuries, with, in some cases, absurd results.

James I planned to import over a million trees to start an English silk industry, and in March 1610 required his Lords Lieutenant to make them available in every county-town of England. But he ordered—we have all made the same mistake—the wrong species. There is hardly an early seventeenth-century house in England without a black mulberry growing in the garden and the nearest the English at that time ever came to sericulture was James and his family feeding silkworms like pets and the Queen winding enough thread to make a taffeta dress to wear on his birthday.

Both species easily predate historic time. Of the two, the white mulberry (*Morus alba*) may be the elder, for more variation exists in the wild. The black mulberry (*Morus nigra*), that can ripen its fruits in the open against a wall as far north as Scotland and southern Sweden, is pretty much unaltered from the wild species that once grew, and still grows, in its original homeland: the forests along the south coast of the Caspian sea, and the high Iranian steppes south of the Caucasus.

It is a tree up to 33ft with a short, rough trunk and spreading branches forming a dense rounded head. The leaves are dark green, with a milky latex in stems and leaves; they look like leaves of nettles (thought to be an herbaceous descendant). Leaves and flowers come late in the spring: when green catkins hang from the mulberry twigs, the frosts should be over. The juicy fruits are raspberry-like, ripening to dark red or purple, even to black, but do not last or travel well, and are usually eaten fresh only *in situ*. In the hill villages of Armenia and Kurdistan, where sugar and vitamins can be hard to come by, they are dried like apricots and figs and preserved in winter cakes. A time-honored way of harvesting them in northern Europe is to spread an old white sheet on the grass and wait for them to drop off.

Black mulberries can live to an enormous age, and easily survive being tipped over by gales (which often happens, because of their dense heads). They simply prop themselves up on their old branches, and come again from the stump. Syon House at Brentford boasts the two oldest trees in England, planted in 1548—they still fruit. A specimen dating from the foundation of the Drapers Hall in 1364 lasted until 1969. Trees planted in the grounds of

MULBERRY NUTCRACKER

19TH CENTURY

Wynyards Antiques London, U.K.

Christ Church, Cambridge and of Stowmarket vicarage in Suffolk by, it is said, John Milton, are teenagers by comparison.

The Greeks and Romans were familiar with the black mulberry from Persia (not the white mulberry, though, for the Chinese jealously hung on to the industrial secret of their silk production) and planted it in their colonizing progress throughout the Mediterranean basin, and, later, when they crossed the Alps into northern Europe. They made wine and cordials from its juice. Black mulberry seeds have been recovered from sites like Silchester and Roman wharfs on the London Thames—probably from trees planted in Britain by the Romans, not imported, because the fruits deteriorate so fast. There is evidence that mulberry trees were also planted on the fringes of the Roman villa at Fishbourne in West Sussex. Mulberry *motifs* turn up in mosaics and frescoes at Pompeii.

The younger Pliny writes in one his letters

MULBERRY: *MORUS NIGRA*, C.1568

J LE MOYNE DE MORGUES
c. 1530–1588
Victoria & Albert Museum London, U.K.

Morus nigra, alba and *rubra*

of the pleasure it gave him to make a stately, litter-borne promenade around the driveway of his country home at Laurentum; an island bed in the middle was planted with figs and mulberries. His uncle, the elder Pliny, who died in A.D. 79, described the tree in his *Historia Naturalis*. The fruits, he wrote, had a wine-like, staining juice, and turned from white to red to black as they ripened; it was one of the last fruit trees to blossom, one of the first to ripen, and it had not been altered a bit by cultivation. The mulberries of Ostia and Tivoli were just the same as those of Rome.

In his *Metamorphoses,* the poet Ovid recalled the myth of Pyramus and Thisbe. Killed in the shade of a mulberry tree, its fruit changed from white to dark red by absorbing their blood.

The Greeks and Romans had heard of silkworms, and had first-hand knowledge of silks and black mulberries (whose leaves will feed the worms, but not nearly so well as those of *Morus alba*), but never connected the three. Silk began arriving in the Mediterranean basin probably after Alexander's eastern campaigns either side of 330 B.C. The Romans could not get enough of the fine, gauzy material that, according to Pliny, did not hide or cover but "showed the body naked." The emperor Tiberius passed a law forbidding men to wear the effeminate material. Its popularity soared. The merchants

MULBERRY TREE, 1889

VINCENT VAN GOGH

1853–1890

Norton Simon Collection

Pasadena, California, U.S.

who brought it on the silk road from China could sell it for its weight in gold.

But how was it made? No one knew, and the Chinese were not telling. Virgil, who died in 19 B.C., thought that it had something to do with mulberry leaves. He was, however, ignorant of the life cycle of the Chinese silk moth, *Bombyx mori*, and how its larva fed on the mulberry tree and spun a cocoon that could be unpicked by patient fingers into up to 1,100 yards of continuous, fine silk thread.

Aristotle, who died in 322 B.C., had heard of a great worm with horns from whose cocoons women separated the threads for spinning. Silk, he thought, was invented on the Aegean island of Cos. His account was the first mention of the silkworm in literature from the West. Pliny the Elder read it and added to it: the luxurious, silken clothes that smart Roman ladies called *bombycina* were made, he wrote, by "silkworms from Assyria." The worms cocooned themselves in round balls of thread and the balls were put in pots and covered with bran to keep them warm, then moistened and unravelled onto a reed spindle. But neither Aristotle nor Pliny mentioned mulberry trees.

Silk-making began in China very early on—records of sericulture date back to the third millennium B.C. Thence it spread to India early in the Christian era—a Chinese princess is supposed to have smuggled in moth larvae and tree seeds concealed in her headdress.

In A.D. 550, two Persian monks who had lived in China came to Emperor Justinian at Constantinople, with details of how silk was made. Justinian packed the monks back off to China and they returned with silkworm eggs hidden in a hollow cane; the cane's contents founded a flourishing silk industry that, over the next 1,200 years, spread slowly, with the white mulberry, throughout western Europe.

You can tell a white mulberry (*Morus alba*) from a black one by its hairless twigs, thin, deeply lobed leaves and stalked fruits (the black's fruits are stalkless). *Alba*'s fruits, when ripe, may be white, pink or purple. Their taste is insipid, and they are not grown for eating.

The prophet Muhammad died in A.D. 632. Within a century of his death, Islam was expanding westwards, and taking with it knowledge of silkworms and white mulberry trees, and planting them in Spain, even in Sicily —twelfth-century Sicilian silks with Islamic patterns still exist. From Sicily, knowledge of sericulture moved north to the Po valley, whose towns became enriched by silk in the Middle Ages, and in 1520 Francis I brought silkworm eggs from Milan to France. By the end of the sixteenth century, Lyon had become a major center of silk production and today in the Rhone valley you can see white mulberries that are left behind by former cultivation, or that have escaped into the wild.

In Britain they are fairly rare outside botanical gardens, but will grow well enough in the open along southern shores.

America has its own native mulberry (*Morus rubra*), a medium-sized tree up to 66ft high, which grows from Massachusetts to Florida, and west to Michigan, but its fruits are disappointing and its leaves are no good for silkworms.

Attempts at sericulture in the New World have all petered out, in spite of government bounties and cajoling over the centuries. Cortes planted mulberries in Mexico in the sixteenth century and James I tried to get an industry going in Virginia as did Benjamin Franklin later in Pennsylvania: all to no avail.

In the 1830s there was a brief craze in North America for a mulberry from the Philippines called *Morus multicaulis*, which was billed by Long Island nurserymen as the answer to the silkworms' prayers. At the height of the fever, huge sums were paid for young plants and nurserymen made fortunes in a single season. But by 1839 the *multicaulis* groves were all gone, wiped out by frost or disease.

Today, one or two hardier individuals survive, the large trees now up to 30 metres (99ft) high: an ironic monument to human folly and greed. The harsh truth is that hand-reeling silk from cocoons is time-consuming and labour-intensive; the profitable silk industries tend to survive in countries like China and India where labour is plentiful and cheap.

In the early 1990s a chemical, deoxynojirimycin, was isolated from the black mulberry by scientists working at Kew Gardens in London. It was found to have an inhibitory effect on the HIV virus and is currently undergoing clinical trials.

WOMEN LINING SHELVES WITH MULBERRY LEAVES FOR SILKWORMS (*top*)

PHILIP GALLE

1537–1612

Private Collection

THE EGGS DULY HATCH INTO WORMS (*bottom*)

PHILIP GALLE

1537–1612

Private Collection

The eggs are covered by mulberry leaves and are placed in branches so the worms weave their cocoons

Fig   *Ficus carica of the* Mulberry *family*

The wild fig, like the olive, originated long before historic time in Asia Minor, then hitched a ride in the stomachs of animals, or with man's cultivation, to become naturalized throughout coastal regions of the Mediterranean and Black Sea basins.

A spreading, deciduous, shrubby tree (up to 23ft tall) with smooth, pale gray bark, you can see it growing today from the Canaries to the Caucasus. It prefers poor ground and seeds itself in unpromising places like cliff cracks, old ruins, stream gorges, cave entrances. It dislikes high mountains, and you can tell it from cultivated varieties by its broad, palmate leaves, which are entire, not deeply lobed, and by its small fruits.

It is the only Mediterranean representative of a vast, thousand-species, tropical and sub-tropical genus that includes huge forest trees, like the aerial rooting banyan of Bengal, and the sacred fig or peepul (*Ficus religiosa*) of Ceylon, beneath whose branches Gautama Buddha is believed to have become a God.

If, as some believe, the flowering plants began their careers millions of years ago as tall, thick-stemmed, tropical trees, then spread out north and south from the equator getting smaller and shrubbier in their colonizing progress, then the wild Mediterranean fig, whose range extends to the Alps, is the descendant of these great equatorial trees.

The wild fig's fruit is mostly small and disappointing, and the first step in its domestication in Asia Minor, long before the art of grafting was introduced to the West from China, was the selection by man of bigger— and fleshier-fruited cultivars that could be "fixed"—i.e. clonally propagated—by taking cuttings of root or stem. The fig, grapevine, olive, pomegranate, and date palm are all easily grown from cuttings too, and these were the first tranche of fruits that were brought into cultivation by man after the invention of grain-farming in the Fertile Crescent—the river lands between the Nile and the Indus—some ten thousand years ago. Fig pips have been found at Neolithic sites, such as Tell Aswad in Syria (7,800–6,600 B.C.) and at Jericho (*c.*7,000 B.C.), but these were probably from wild fruits collected by hunter gatherers. However, carbonized pips found at sites in the Jordan valley and Dead Sea area, dating from about 3,500 B.C., are thought to be from cultivated figs, and evidence from Sumerian clay writing tablets makes it certain they were being grown in Mesopotamia one thousand years later. One medical tablet recommends mixing dried, pulverized thyme,

And the eyes
of them both
were opened,
and they
knew that
they were
naked; and
they sewed
fig leaves
together; and
made
themselves
aprons.

Genesis 3:6,7

Fig Wood Carved
Figure

(detail)

Egyptian, Middle
Kingdom

twelfth dynasty

Louvre, Paris, France

indeed, and unique to the genus. The fruit is not really a fruit at all, but a hollow, fleshy, inward-curving receptacle containing many tiny flowers that are pollinated, and ripen their seeds, on the inside without ever seeing the light. Wild plants are either exclusively male (called "caprifigs") or female ("true figs"); the fruits of the females soon drop to the ground, small and unregarded, if they are not pollinated by male trees: no easy matter when the only access to the hidden female flowers is via a tiny hole in the non-twig end of the receptacle. An elaborate symbiosis with the tiny fig wasp *Blastophaga psenes*, however, does the trick every time: the wasp's eggs are laid, and its larvae nourished in winter, within the smaller caprifig fruits of male trees, then pollen-carrying adult wasps fly to the female trees in early summer and crawl in through the tiny holes.

This process, known as "caprification," was well known to the ancients, at least as early as Greek classical times. In early summer the Greeks hung pollinating branches cut from wild caprifigs in their (mostly female) orchards to achieve fruit set. Today, growers of the delicious "Smyrna" fig varieties (they are "dioecious"—wholly male or female) have to practice this same, ancient art. The alternative is to grow one of the five hundred-odd varieties of Common or Adriatic fig, whose parthenocarpic fruits, after centuries of cultivation and selection, have made the fig wasp redundant: they swell on the branch and mature without any need for pollination.

The figs of Attica, like its olives, were famous throughout the ancient world, and helped to make Athens rich. Cultivated varieties had been introduced, it was believed, from Caria (the modern southwest Turkey

pears and figs with beer and oil, and using the paste as a poultice. Figs are recorded in Egypt from about 2,750 B.C, and a drawing of a fig harvest from 1,900 B.C was found in Knumhotep's grave in Beni Hasan.

A problem for early fig growers was sorting out the botany of the fruit, which is very odd

opposite Rhodes): hence the specific name. If you ate at the public tables in Sparta it was just about all you got to eat, and Greek athletes, to build up speed and strength, liked to train on a fig-only diet. Figs were so popular that their export was regulated by law. An informer against a fig export lawbreaker was called a *sukophantes*, from *sukon*, a fig, and *phainein*, to make known—whence the English word sycophant derives.

When were figs first cultivated in Greece? Remains dating from the late Bronze Age (1,250 B.C.) have been found at Pylos in the Peloponnese, and in a Minoan palace storehouse on Crete; but whether they were wild or cultivated, homegrown or imported, it is hard to say. Homer (about 1,000 B.C.) mentions a fig tree in the *Iliad* that grew near Troy, and in the *Odyssey* they feature in the fabulous gardens of Alcinous, King of Phaeacia (perhaps the modern Corfu), and dangle over the head of poor, tortured Tantalus in the underworld: "And each time the old man stood up to grab at them, the wind blew them away to the shadowy clouds." But Homer, otherwise keen on gardening, seems ignorant of how to grow them. The lyric poet Archilochus was the first Greek to describe their culture on his home island of Paros in the 650s B.C. By the time of the Persian wars in the fifth century B.C., the cultivated fruit was well established on the mainland as were wild figs, which the Greeks called *erineoi*.

The fig sailed to Italy, Spain and North Africa with Greek and Phoenicean colonists; by Roman times it was being grown all round the Mediterranean basin. Pliny the Elder, who died in the great eruption of Vesuvius that buried Pompeii in A.D. 79, detailed twenty-nine different varieties, and said the best ones (they still do) came from Turkey and, much nearer at home, from Herculaneum near Naples. Two centuries earlier, Cato the Censor had brandished fresh Carthaginian figs in the Roman senate to demonstrate the proximity of the hated enemy city in North Africa.

In Pliny's day, agricultural slave workers in Italy were fed mainly on a diet of figs, both fresh and dried, and the Roman legionary on active service ate dried figs on the march. Doctors prescribed figs for constipation, and Roman gardeners grew figs not only for their fruit, but for their shape and shade.

The younger Pliny, nephew of the naturalist, built a circular driveway in front of his villa at Laurentum, around which, when the weather was fine, he made stately, litter-borne promenades; an island bed in the middle was planted with mulberries and figs. At the Villa Poppea at Oplontis, a fresco of a wicker-

FRESCO OF A BASKET OF FIGS

FIRST CENTURY A.D.
Villa Poppea
Oplontis, Italy

basketful of figs looks as fresh as when they were painted two thousand years ago.

Figs featured in Roman myth and in Roman, Jewish and early Christian religion. The God Saturn was believed to have discovered the fruit; the inhabitants of Cyrene in North Africa wore wreaths of fig leaves when they sacrificed to him. Romulus and Remus, founders of Rome, were suckled by a wolf under a fig tree, which was afterwards held sacred by her citizens. On the first day of the year Romans gave figs to each other as presents. In St Mark's gospel (XI. 13–14; 21–22) there is the strange story of the fig tree inexplicably cursed by Jesus after his triumphant ride into Jerusalem:

And seeing a fig tree afar off having leaves, he came, if haply he might find anything thereon: and when he came to it, he found nothing but leaves; for the time of figs was not yet.
And Jesus answered and said unto it, No man eat fruit of thee hereafter for ever.

Later, the apostle Peter pointed out the tree, which had shrivelled and died. Jesus' answer was enigmatic: "Have faith in God." Perhaps he was prejudiced by Jewish suspicions that the fig was the Tree of Knowledge; his curse certainly has a Genesis ring to it. In the Old Testament, Hezekiah had no such qualms and he allowed a servant to cure his boil by applying a fig cake poultice.

Cultivated figs can be ripened outside in sunny, sheltered spots in Britain and Germany, but wild figs stopped firmly at the Alps and so did the Mediterranean's enthusiasm for the fruit as a poor man's staple. Fig seeds that had probably been imported have been recovered from Roman wharf sites on the Thames and Charlemagne included figs in a list of favorite fruits from A.D. 800.

Nevertheless, until about the eighteenth century the common man in northern Europe was deeply suspicious of fresh fruit, unless he could actually pick it off a tree. Figs were best left to rich eccentrics: to men like Thomas à Becket, who is said to have planted a fig orchard of five hundred trees at West Tarring, near Worthing in Sussex in 1145; or to the wife of Edward I, who bought a basket of figs off a cargo ship from Spain, or even to Cardinal Pole who, some say, planted the first fig tree in England at Lambeth Palace in about 1525. This tree was still fruiting well two hundred years later, according to Philip Miller, who was head of the Apothecaries' Garden at Chelsea and helped to put the fig on the English horticultural map in the eighteenth century. He imported and tested many new cultivars, sent to him by a contact in Venice; among them was the still popular Brown Turkey.

Figs were unknown in the Americas before Columbus, but Spanish colonists were soon growing them in the New World. Pedro Cicza de Léon was a boy soldier from Seville who spent seventeen years in South America from 1535 onwards. In his *Chronicle of Peru*, he wrote of the large fig groves he had seen on the irrigated plains round the recently founded Lima.

In the eighteenth century, figs were introduced by Jesuit missionaries to California, where, today, there is a sophisticated export trade in fresh, canned and dried figs, as well as in fig paste and syrup.

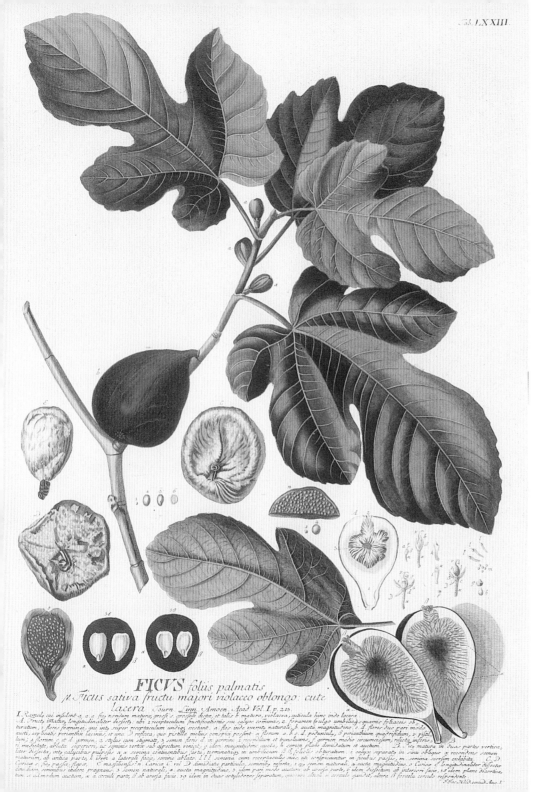

Tab. LXXIII.

FICVS *foliis palmatis*
* β Ficus sativa fructu majori violaceo oblongo: cute*
lacera Tourn. Linn. Amoen. Acad. Vol. I. p. 243.

BOTANICAL
ENGRAVING OF
THE FIG, PLATE 73

JOHANN JAKOB HAID
1704–1767
Private Collection

Melons & watermelons

Cucumis melo *and* Citrullus lanatus *of the* Marrow *family*

The cucurbits and their origins—Pliny the Elder first used the word *Cucurbita*, meaning a gourd, in his *Naturalis Historia* from A.D. 77—have had botanists in terrible tangles over the years, from Gerard's 1597 *Herball,* right up to the twentieth century. Difficulties have arisen over identifying and naming: melons often resemble squashes and one man's pumpkin tends to be another man's gourd.

One easy distinction is that of the most important cucurbits grown and eaten by man, cucumbers, gherkins (which are cucumbers picked very small), melons, and watermelons come from the Old World (Europe, Asia, and Africa). Pumpkins, squashes, marrows, and zucchini originate in the New World (North and South America). Hard-skinned, strong-tendriled gourds are mostly New World plants, but there are exceptions: the Bottle Gourd or Calabash, *Lagenaria vulgaris*, from Africa, is halved and used as a goblet from which to drink palm wine, or left whole it is employed to teach children to swim, the cucumber-like Snake Gourd from tropical Asia, *Trichosanthes cucumeriana*, turns from green to bright red as it ripens; and the large (up to 30lbs and 5ft long) cylindrical Wax Gourd from Java, *Benincasa hispida*, prized in Asian cuisine, is available nowadays to Western cooks.

The center of origin of the melon (*Cucumis melo*) is Africa. Wild melon populations grow from south of the Sahara as far as the Transvaal. In West Africa they have been found growing in sand on the banks of the river Niger. It is considered likely that they were first domesticated by Africans, even by our tool-using ancestor, *Homo habilis*, who emerged into the Levant some two million years ago. Other wild melon populations occur from Asia Minor, through Afghanistan and India to China, but these may well derive from ancient wildings—prehistoric escapes from the gardens (or, more likely, middens) of early out-of-Africa man.

Wild melons are tropical or subtropical, trailing, weedy, annual plants with small, plum-sized variable fruits from which a bewildering number of cultivars have evolved. There are summer muskmelons or cantaloups (medium-sized with netted, scaly skins and mostly orange, sweetly scented flesh); winter or honeydew melons (large with smooth or wrinkled skin and white or green flesh, less scented); chitos, dudaims, and conomons (small, mostly bitter melons used for pickling and preserves, especially in India); serpent melons (also called Armenian melons) which are eaten immature like cucumbers; and snap

Cucumis melo and *Citrullus lanatus*

melons with smooth skins and white or pale orange flesh. Many are interfertile, both with each other and with the wild species, so the potential for hybridization has been, and remains, great. In world production terms, the two most important cultivars are the muskmelons and the honeydews.

Early archaeological evidence for melons is scanty. Three carbonized seeds have been identified at Tiryns, three miles from the sea in the marshy plain of Argolis, dating from the Greek late Bronze Age (*c.*1,000 B.C.). Other seeds, found in eastern Iran, may be a thousand years older.

The Sumerians, a wandering tribe who settled in Mesopotamia in the fourth millennium B.C., called the melon *ukus*; but whether they meant the small, bitter "finger" melon, or the larger, sweet melon is unclear. Bent, green-skinned, cucumber-like fruits also feature in Egyptian tomb paintings, notably in the Tomb of Nakht (*c.*1,400 B.C.) at Western Thebes. These, despite appearances, were probably not cucumbers, but bitter, edible-when-cooked, pickling melons.

The cucumber (*Cucumis sativus*) occurs in the wild only in the Himalayas and in lands to the east of those mountains. It is thought to have been domesticated first in northern India, and to have arrived in the Mediterranean basin rather late, sometime around the middle of the first millennium B.C. and too late for the Egyptian tombs. The earliest evidence for cucumbers in the Near East—two seeds of *sativus*, dated to about 600 B.C.—comes from Nimrud in Iraq.

When did sweet melons arrive in the West? A Chinese origin is hard to prove, but both sweet muskmelons and bitter pickling melons do feature in early Chinese literature—the Shih Ching, a Chinese anthology of the first millennium B.C., contains detailed descriptions—and the fruit has been very much a part of Chinese horticulture ever since.

The Greeks had a fruit they ate ripe called *sikua* or *pepon* or *melopepon* and one or other of these may have been a muskmelon. Galen, a medical writer who came to Rome from Asia Minor in about A.D. 160, wrote that the insides of *melopepones*, but not of *pepones*, were edible, so the likeliest candidate for muskmelon, if it was grown at all, seems to be *melopepon*.

Translated from the Greek it means "apple-melon" It must have been a poor plant compared to present-day cultivars, for there is not a word of praise for so delicious a fruit in any of the classical gardening authors like Virgil, Pliny, Varro or Columella. It does, however, appear in a Vatican Roman mosaic.

Wilifrid Strabo, poet and abbot of the

Benedictine monastery at Reichenau, situated on an island in Lake Constance in the ninth century A.D., probably had the muskmelon or the watermelon in mind when he described it in his *Hortulus*, as:

. . . the spoil and chief pride
Of a garden, a choice and delectable feast
That will tickle your palate, yet not in the least
Set your teeth upon edge.
Down it slips like a dream,
And refreshes your soul with its icy-cool stream.

The suspicion remains, though, that the widespread culture of muskmelons, like that of oranges and lemons, was introduced to the Mediterranean basin by the growth of Islam in the eightth century A.D. Muskmelons require 65°F to germinate and 75–80°F to ripen, so they would have enjoyed the trip from Asia along the north coast of Africa and into Spain, thence to Sicily, Italy and France where, in the fifteenth century, they were enthusiastically grown by the Avignon Popes. At the end of the thirteenth century Marco

Polo wrote that the best melons in the world, were sold in huge quantities in a city he called Shibarghan (today known as Sapurgan in Afghanistan):

They dry them in this manner. They cut them all round in slices like strips of leather, then put them in the sun to dry, when they become sweeter than honey...they are easily sold in the countryside around.

Melons were not grown in England until the late 1500s when the tender new plants pouring in from the New World and Asia encouraged gardeners to experiment with hotbeds and protection under glass. John Gerard illustrated and described several kinds of melons, which wrongly he called gourds, in his 1597 *Herball*. There were no melons in the New World before Columbus, but on his 1494 expedition he took seeds with him and planted them on Haiti. The fruits, he claimed, did so well that they were ready to eat within two months. They have been doing well in the American tropics and subtropics ever since.

Cantaloup muskmelons take their name from the town of Cantalupo near Rome,

Cucumis melo and *Citrullus lanatus*

where they were grown in abundance on the papal estates, and later, in the nineteenth century, in market gardens on the fringes of Paris. They are slightly elongated, with pale green or golden skins, often netted and marked into segments, and their orange-yellow flesh smells (and tastes) delicious. Alexandre Dumas considered them the best of all melons provided that they "had been caressed by the rays of the sun." He recommended eating a cantaloup with pepper and salt, and washing it down with a half glass of Marsala or Madeira.

The only cucurbit native to the British Isles is the vine-like White Bryony (*Bryonia dioica*), which sprawls through the hedges. Do not try eating its red berries, though, as a cucumber or melon substitute. They are poisonous and will give even goats a stomachache.

The Watermelon (*Citrullus lanatus*) grows wild in tropical and southern Africa. Kalahari bushmen—they call it *tsama*—have used it for centuries as a source of water and food (not much in the flesh except water, but its edible seeds are full of oil, protein and fiber). In the Kalahari there are both bitter and non-bitter varieties. It is believed that the watermelon's ancestor may well be the wild, trailing perennial Colocynth or Bitter Gourd (*Citrullus colocynthis*) with which it is fully interfertile. Bitter Gourds grow in the desert sands of North Africa and Western Asia, and nomads still collect their small, intensely bitter, spongy fruits and use them as purgatives, or even as food. Their distinctive small seeds have turned up in very early (4,000 B.C.) archaeological sites in both Israel and the Nile valley and it is thought Bitter Gourds were gathered in the wild long before they were improved by domestication and turned into watermelons, whose larger seeds turn up much later: at sites that date from 2,000 B.C. in Egypt, for example, and in the tomb of Tutankhamun, dating from 1,325 B.C.

Watermelons do not seem to have reached China until about the end of the first millennium A.D. They rarely feature in western literature or art before the Renaissance. From the fifteenth century onwards, of course, their juicy red flesh, black seeds and distinctive shape and size made them great favorites with painters of still lives. Like muskmelons, they became popular in western Europe following the eighth-century advance of Islam. Today, they are grown all round the world, on the largest land area and with the biggest tonnage of all the cucurbits.

China is the world's premier producer of watermelons; other major growers are Turkey and the former USSR.

RUSSIAN PORCELAIN "PROPAGANDA" PLATE, 1921

STATE PORCELAIN FACTORY

Dreweatt Neate Fine Art Auctioneers, Newbury Berkshire, U.K.

Cucumis melo and *Citrullus lanatus*   79

Kiwifruit

Actinidia deliciosa *of the* Yang Tao *family*

Until the final years of the last century, *Actinidia deliciosa* was a wild perennial vine that grew in rampant profusion over the hills and mountains of southwest China, in the region where the flow of the river West, in the south, and the Yangste, in the middle of China, drain down out of the eastern Himalayas.

Every autumn, when its fruits were ripe, Chinese peasants would go out to the hills in droves and pick vast quantities for eating and selling in their markets. They had done so since time immemorial. Texts dating from the Tang dynasty (A.D. 618–960) confirm that even then it was already an old custom for peasants to gather the fruits they called *mihoutao* or *yangtao*, which roughly means "monkey-peach," in the mountains. During the harvest season, it was a race with the macaque monkeys of the Chinese hill forests over who would get the fruits first.

There was never any need to farm the vine. Woody, deciduous and very vigorous, it clambers up to 28ft over hillside shrubs and trees at will and grows vast quantities of large, oblong, brownish, bristly, fruits filled with greenish pulp and delicious grape-like juice. The seeds are small and black, and easily digestible.

Very much to its liking are the mountains of inland Yunnan province, where it rains hard and regularly throughout the year, and there is a frost-free growing season of seven or eight months, followed by winter chilling—the plants need at least four hundred hours below 42°F to encourage flower production. Here,

too, grow most of the other sixty-odd species of *Actinidia* so far identified by botanists. A few grow farther afield in India, Japan, Korea, Indonesia, even in Siberia.

A. chinensis, which some Chinese rate above *deliciosa*, has smaller, rounder fruit covered with soft peach-like fur, and perhaps a more delicate flavor. It is a very close relation of *deliciosa* that has adapted to the lower elevations and warmer temperatures in the east of China, towards the South China Sea.

Actinidia still grows in profusion in China and the Chinese still pick it for free, like blackberries in Europe, and in incredible quantities. An annual figure of some 200,000 tons has been estimated. But its status as a wild food, locally consumed, changed for ever in 1899 when an English planthunter, Ernest Henry "Chinese" Wilson, came to China and began sending seeds home to Veitch's nursery in Chelsea, England. New plants from China were much in demand at the time, and gardeners in the West were keen to grow what they called "Chinese gooseberries" as ornamental vines in outdoor, temperate conditions, to scramble up trees or over pergolas, or cover stumps. Ornamental, mostly, they remained.

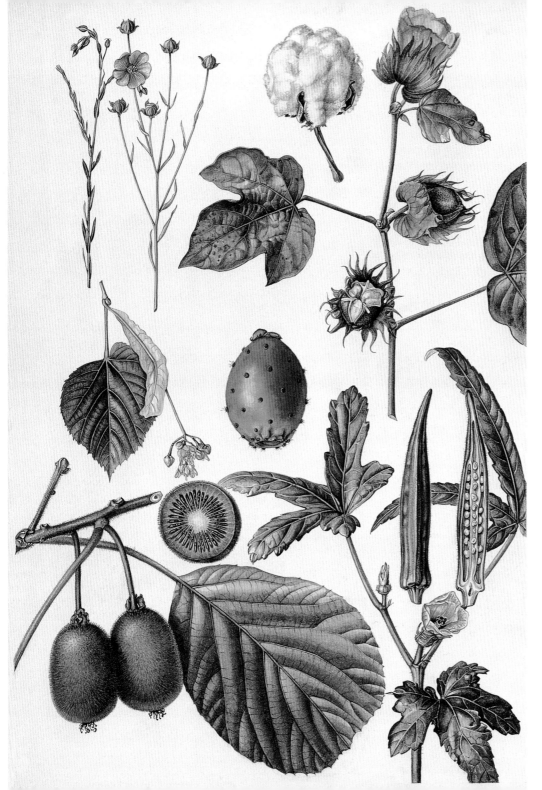

KIWI FRUIT AND OTHER PLANTS
ELIZABETH RICE
Watercolor on paper
Private Collection

Actinidia deliciosa

DR. HAYWARD WRIGHT, 1933 *(right)*
The Hayward cultivar was named after the plant selector and nurseryman

CHINESE GOOSEBERRY PACKAGING, COVENT GARDEN, 1953 *(opposite)*
The fruit was called Chinese Gooseberry in New Zealand in 1917, before it changed to Kiwifruit in 1959, a named devised for export to the U.S.

Actinidia are all dioecious, that is, you need two simultaneously flowering plants, one male and the other female, to achieve successful flower pollination and fruiting. *Deliciosa* is much easier to grow in temperate gardens than the softer *chinensis,* and soon became the preferred species.

In 1904, the first seeds of *deliciosa* were sent to New Zealand, where they successfully germinated to produce three vines: two female and one male. In the 1920s, scions of these plants, of determined sex and fruiting quality, were being grafted, and by the early 1930s the world's first commercial kiwifruit orchard was established—although the fruit did not get its new name until 1959, when New Zealand farmers, realizing its potential, laid plans for a sustained campaign of culture, advertising and export. Plants were found to bear fruit three to four years after planting, they needed stout support on a T-frame or pergola and required careful pruning and training to promote fruit growth. Ten percent of an orchard needed to be male plants to ensure adequate pollination and it was discovered that growing plants detested the wind and hail.

In about 1930, Hayward Wright selected a female plant from a row of forty seedlings (only one or two generations removed from the seeds imported in 1904), to be grown as the "Hayward" cultivar, which would enable kiwifruit to be sold all over the world as a fresh-fruit rival to oranges, peaches or plums.

One kiwi contains more than one hundred percent of the recommended daily intake of vitamin C and it is high in vitamin E, potassium, dietary fiber, and folic acid (good for pregnant women and adolescents). It has excellent flavor and keeping qualities: up to several months if properly wrapped and chilled. When New

Zealand exports of kiwifruit began rapidly to expand in the 1970s it was the only cultivar that shippers wanted in their holds.

Today, "Hayward" is farmed in California, Chile, Japan, France, Spain, South Africa and Italy and annual world production is about 650,000 tons. In China, too, where it all began, the culture is rapidly expanding. Italy and New Zealand are the world's major producers. In a single century, the Chinese monkey peach of the Himalayan hinterland has become the famous kiwi, familiar to supermarket shoppers right round the world.

Pomegranate

Punica granatum *of the* Pomegranate *family*

The pomegranate is an ancient plant, cultivated since time immemorial. For thirsty men in desert places it provided refreshing, sweet-sour juice long before the squeezing of oranges, lemons or tangerines. The earliest sherbet was pomegranate juice mixed with snow.

POMEGRANATE

(opposite)

JOHANN JAKOB HAID
1704–1767
Colored engraving
Private Collection

**ROUNDEL FROM
ROMAN VILLA,
HINTON ST. MARY**

ROMAN MOSAIC
FOURTH CENTURY A.D.
*Dorset County
Museum, U.K.*

The wild pomegranate probably originated in northern Persia. It spread out from there in prehistoric times, its seeds dispersed by birds or planted by the first farmers: east as far as China, where it has been cultivated since pre-Christian times and west into Turkey, Greece and the Levant and along the North African littoral as far as the Canaries. A good place to see the wild species is on dry, stony hillsides south of the Caspian Sea, where it still grows in profusion.

Botanically, it is a strange plant: taxonomists are unable even to agree into which family it belongs. Some say the loosestrifes, others the myrtles, others give it a family all of its own, the pomegranates (*Punicaceae*). Its carpels (part of the flower's ovary) are set in two rows, which is extremely rare. One row lies above the other and faces the opposite way to the first. A second species—the pomegranate is a two-species genus and a one-genus family—

grows only on the island of Socotra, two hundred miles off the Horn of Africa in the Gulf of Aden; it has a single-level carpel row.

In the wild it is a bush or small tree, up to about 16.5ft tall—with a straight, reddish-brown trunk and spreading branches with glossy, green, lance-shaped leaves that turn yellow and die in the autumn (in the tropics, they stay evergreen). The flowers are a bright, waxy scarlet and the deep yellow fruits, about the size of a small orange, are topped off with a persistent calyx that resembles a tall, medieval crown which became a symbol of kingship in the Middle Ages: Henry IV adopted the pomegranate from the Moorish kings as his heraldic emblem, with the motto "Sour, yet sweet," and it was Catherine of Aragon's device when she married Henry VIII. At a court ball in her honor, roses and pomegranates acknowledged the union of England and Spain.

The fruit—botanically, it is a berry—has a thick, leathery rind that encloses many seeds set in pink, juicy pulp. Wild or half-wild fruits tend to be smaller and contain less juice than those improved by cultivation. They were among the first fruits to be brought into

Punica granatum

Tab. LXXII.

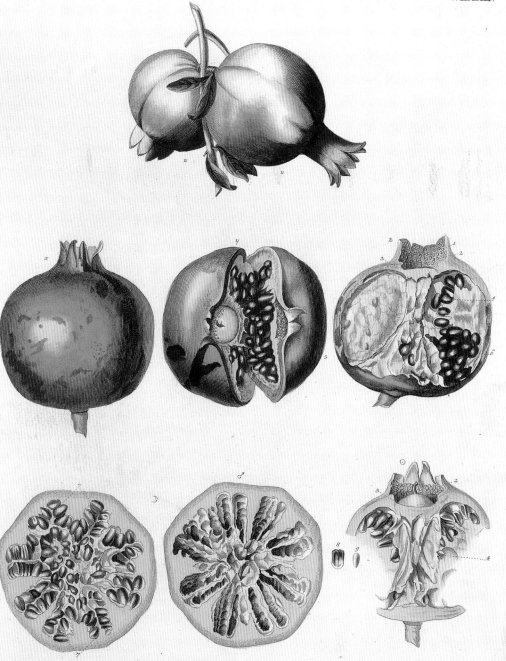

PVNICÆ n°. I. *Tab. LXXI.* *Poma* seu *Punica mala*.

u. u. Poma maturescentia ramulo insidentia, x. fructus maturus, integer. y sponte ruptus, z. ⊙. verticaliter dissectus: ubi notantur, 1. calycis segmentum cum staminibus aridis, 2. 2. stylus et stigma, 3. 3. operculum consessum, 4. 4. styli per medium fructus continuatio, 5. membrana pollucida, loculos et seminibus intergerina, 6. eadem remota, loculos et granis denudatis. ⊅. Pomum horizontaliter dissectum, 7. 7. loculi seminibus repleti, 6. ab iisde evacuati, 8. granum involucro suo ambitum, 9. idem nudum.

And Saul tarried in the uttermost part of Gibeah under a pomegranate tree which is in Migron . . .

Samuel 14:2

cultivation after grain-farming was invented in the Fertile Crescent—the river lands between the Nile and the Indus—about ten thousand years ago. References to pomegranates turn up on Mesopotamian cuneiform writing tablets (2,500 B.C.), and similarly dated carbonized pips and fragments of rind of what were probably cultivated pomegranates have been identified at Jericho in the Jordan valley, about five miles north of the Dead Sea. Pomegranates are not native to, only naturalized in, the southern Levant; archaeologists suspect their culture in the Near East may predate the first archaeological evidence for their presence there by hundreds, perhaps thousands, of years. Traces of pips and rind have been found in Egypt (about 1,800 B.C.) and levels dating to 1,500 B.C. in Greece and Cyprus (where, according to myth, the Greek goddess of love, Aphrodite, introduced the first pomegranate). A complete, desiccated pomegranate was recovered from the tomb of Djehuty, butler to the Egyptian Queen Hatshepsut in about 1,470 B.C.

It is often represented on ancient Assyrian, Egyptian and Greek sculptures—there is a lovely Parian marble relief (the *Stele l'exaltation de la fleur*) in the Louvre, showing two women facing each other and holding what are thought to be pomegranate flowers. By about the middle of the second millennium B.C. it seems to have established itself as a fairly common fruit throughout eastern Mediterranean lands and to have spread east into India and Asia, arriving in China as a cultivated fruit sometime before the Christian era. In Arabic it was called *rumman*, in Sanskrit *darimba*, in Greek *roa*, in Hebrew (in the Old Testament) *rimmon*. It was one of the fruits of the Promised Land of the Bible, and was used as a motif on the sculpted pillars of King Solomon's temple, and on the embroidered hem of the High Priest's surplice. Homer was familiar with pomegranates. He mentioned them twice in the *Odyssey* (he called them *roai*), written around 800 B.C.

The Romans tended to name fruit and vegetables after the place in which they thought they originated; in the case of pomegranates, Carthage in North Africa. They called them *mala punica*, Punic apples, and grew them in their villa gardens in Italy. But these must have been garden cultivars, not wild species, that had spread along the Mediterranean coastline via Egypt from the Levant, and had probably been introduced to Carthage by Phoenician or Greek colonists long before the Romans had anything to do with the town. The Romans enjoyed the pomegranate as a fresh summer fruit, as well as using it as a vermifuge (wormer), its bark as a tanning agent for leather and its leaves and seeds to treat diarrhea. They planted it, along with pears, apples, peaches, quinces, cherries and almonds to make cool, shady rooms in the quincunx-pattern courtyards of their town houses at Pompeii, later buried by the eruption of Vesuvius in A.D. 79. The Romans loved too, to paint trompe l'oeil garden scenes, actual or mythical, as frescos on their villa walls. You can see pomegranates featured in the House of the Fruit Orchard at Pompeii, and pomegranates and quinces flank a pine tree in a fresco in the House of Livia at Primaporta, Rome.

The pomegranate was a symbol of fertility in the myths and religions of the ancient world—in Persia it was, and still is, a centuries-old custom for brides to squash a pomegranate underfoot before entering their new home, to ensure children. The fruit was associated with the cults of Aphrodite, Dionysus and Persephone in Greece; and, particularly, with the cult of Cybele, the Great Mother of the Gods, that arose in Asia Minor in the Greek Dark Ages and persisted well into Roman imperial times—it was one of the last pagan cults to die after Christianity was made legal by Constantine in A.D. 312.

Early Christians borrowed the Mother-of-God idea of the Cybele cult, but bowdlerized its pagan symbolism, substituting fidelity for fertility. The pomegranate became a Christian sign, like the Chi Rho symbol, equally applied, it seems, to Mother and Son: a head of Jesus that dates from the fourth century A.D. flanked by two pomegranates was uncovered in 1963 on a Roman villa floor at Hinton St Mary, near Shaftesbury in Dorset. The mosaic is now in the British Museum. This has great significance, especially when one remembers that St Augustine and his forty monks did not arrive in Kent to Christianise Britain until A.D. 597. Renaissance painters like Botticelli, Filippo Lippi and Fra Angelico all depicted the Holy Family either holding, or being offered, pomegranates as tokens of devotion and love.

Pomegranates like dry, hot climates, with temperatures of 96°F needed for fruiting. In northern Europe they rarely fruit and are mostly grown for their flowers. Following the voyages of discovery in the fifteenth and

sixteenth centuries, the tropics and subtropics of the New World beckoned as ideal habitats.

Today, pomegranates are grown in most tropical and subtropical countries, but they have become a relatively minor crop, their ancient popularity as a thirst-quenching fruit usurped in the West by cultivars of citrus and melon. In the souks of Istanbul, however, you can still drink the tart juice of the pomegranate from silver cups. Cocktails, like tequila sunrise are still made with a base of grenadine (pomegranate syrup) and a favorite non-alcoholic drink in French cafés is grenadine with soda and ice.

PERSEPHONE IN THE UNDERWORLD

VIRGINIA FRANCES STERRETT

Persephone, who is abducted by Hades, eats six pomegranate seeds and must thereafter spend six months of each year in the Underworld, thus bringing Winter to the world of Man

And Noah began to be an husbandman, and he planted a vineyard. And he drank of the wine and he was drunken; and he was uncovered within his tent.

Genesis IX,20

Grapevine

Vitis vinifera *of the* Vine *family*

Noah was not the first man to get drunk, then collapse into bed in a naked heap. If, as palaeontologists now believe, *Homo habilis*, the predecessor of *erectus*, emerged from Africa two million years ago and lived in the open, in the Levant, he may have encountered *Vitis vinifera silvestris*.

These rather small and acidic, but juicy, berries contain enough sugar to make drinkable wine. He had only to encounter fermenting berries—a pile in the forest perhaps, or set aside in a stone or wooden dish (in the 1990s, two-million-year-old knives and chopping tools of basalt, flint and limestone belonging to *habilis* were excavated in a dry river-bed south of the Sea of Galilee at Erq-Lel-Ahmar)—and *habilis* could have beaten Noah to it by a distance.

Nudity in tents would not have bothered him: *habilis* had no tent and wore no clothes. And if he never got drunk—the wild grape did not and does not grow in the hot, dry Jordan valley where the tools were found—then his hunter gathering, wider-ranging successor in the Middle East about 1.5 million years ago, *Homo erectus*, must surely have had better luck.

Nowadays, the true range of the wild grape, from which nearly all cultivated grapes derive, is rather blurred by vineyard escapes reverted to the wild (what the Germans call, in a lovely phrase, *werwildert*, and the English, more prosaically, *sub-spontaneous*). It is the only Eurasian representative of the sixty-species

Vitis genus. All the others grow in North America—especially in Florida and southeastern States—or in eastern Asia. *Vinifera*, the Eurasian species, is a rampant, woody vine with stems up to 66ft long, that attach themselves to host trees and shrubs by tendrils. It likes hot summers and cool wet winters, and you can find it growing in the northern hemisphere from the Spanish Atlantic coast to the Himalayas, in the north up the Rhone, Rhine and Danube, and in the south along the moister, coastal shores of North Africa, Egypt and the Middle East.

The wild vine originated, it is thought, in central Asia, in the tall, temperate forests that rimmed the southern shores of the Black and Caspian seas. It still grows there, in the region the ancients called Armenia, Media and Parthia, and you can see it scrambling through wild poplars, figs, willows, pears or plums, supported by whose branches and, without benefit of the pruning knife, it fruits abundantly. In the wild it is what botanists call "dioecious": plants are male or female in about a 50:50 ratio, and need to grow near each other to achieve fruit set and pollination. Most

THE STORY OF NOAH: THE EXODUS FROM THE ARK, THE DRUNKENNESS OF NOAH AND HIS SACRIFICE TO GOD, 1425–1452

LORENZO GHIBERTI
1378–1455
Gilt Bronze
From The Gates of Paradise (East Doors)
Baptistry, Florence, Italy

fig, was included in the first tranche of fruits that they were bringing in from the wild and growing in their garden plots. They used vine cuttings—and thus clonally "fixed" desired genotypes, generation after generation: vine seedlings produced by sexual pollination tend to be recessive.

Knowledge of grafting, which did not arrive from China until about 1,000 B.C., was not a requirement. Other fruits like apples, pears, plums, and cherries, whose culture is dependent on grafting, did not emerge in the Mediterranean basin until that date.

Archaeologists can just about distinguish between pips from wild and cultivated grapes; wild grape pips under the microscope tend to be more oval and less elongated, with pronounced, beaky stalks. Numerous carbonized wild grape pips, and occasionally whole grapes, have been found in Stone Age sites from Germany, through France, Switzerland and the Balkans, to Greece and Cyprus: thus confirming the extensive range of wild *vinifera silvestris*, and its use as food by hunter gatherers.

The first definite archaeological evidence of vine cultivation comes from an area where we know it did not grow wild: a chalcolithic (*c.*3,500 B.C.) site in the Jordan valley and in Early Bronze Age (3,200 B.C.) levels at Jericho. A dig at nearby Arad yielded two pieces of charred grape wood in contemporary levels. But the Jordan pips were round and beaky, of the wild type. Were the grapes and wood imported from elsewhere? The likeliest explanation is that primitive cultivars were grown on the spot, using irrigation.

The first literary evidence for wine making comes from a clay cuneiform tablet of the

modern cultivars are hermaphroditic, and can fertilise themselves, with pistils and anthers all on the same plant.

The first viticulture, as the forests were gradually opened up by hunter gathering tribes, may have involved nothing more than not cutting down a certain tree that supported a good specimen of grapevine, and marking it and declaring it taboo.

By about 8,000 B.C., when the first farmers were living more or less sedentary lives in the fertile river lands between the Tigris and Euphrates, the grapevine, along with the olive, pomegranate, date palm and

Sumerians. They were wanderers who settled in southern Iraq in about 3,500 B.C. and founded the urban civilisation that later came to be known as Babylon. One tablet records a mock dispute between summer (*emesh*) and winter (*enten*) and enumerates the delights that a good summer can produce:

In the plain he made rejoice the heart of the wild goat, sheep and donkey...in the [date] palm grove he made honey and wine abound. The trees, wherever planted, he caused to bear fruit.

By the beginning of the second millennium B.C. evidence of grape cultivation and wine drinking along the eastern Mediterranean rim and in the Middle East comes thick and fast. The Phoenicians, the great seafarers and traders of the ancient world, who came from the coastal regions of modern Syria and Lebanon, took wine and knowledge of viticulture to Spain, Sicily and Italy, and the coast of North Africa and Egypt. Rich Egyptians (poor Egyptians lived on bread and onions, washed down with beer made from barley dough soaked in date-sweetened water) were importing wine from about 3,000 B.C., first as funerary wine, then drinking it and making it in vineyards in the Nile Delta by at least the second millennium.

There is a marvelous series of viticultural wall paintings in the tomb of Nakht, in the Valley of the Kings near Luxor. Nakht was some sort of middle-ranking official of the Thutmose era (*c.*1,400 B.C.). His tomb paintings depict life on the farm in ancient Egypt. Bunches of grapes are picked and trodden in a tub by men steadying themselves with ropes, while another drains the pressed juice through a spigot into amphorae and stacks the jars on shelves.

In Roman times, the white, sweet Mareotic wine from the Nile's delta, according to Athenaeus "good for the breath and digestible," was famous throughout the ancient world and was exported everywhere. Egyptian wine buffs would store jars for anything up to 200 years, carefully sealed and labeled, and lyricize about the best vintages.

Then, in the seventh century A.D., when Moslem hordes of the Ummayad Caliphate swept into Egypt and along the North African coast, they lost everything—vineyards, winepresses and cellars. The grape, according to the prophet Muhammad, was an abomination. Every vineyard was replaced with citrus fruit orchards, but they were but a small consolation.

There were ways to circumnavigate the ban, of course: Marco Polo visited Persia and came across Saracens drinking heated, sweetened wine, which they called something else.

Byblos was a seaside town in Phoenicia (the modern Lebanon). In the Aegean late Bronze Age, *c.*1,000 B.C., Lebanese wine was very good, just as it is nowadays. Hesiod, the poet from the eighth

ATTIC RED-FIGURE STAMNOS, DECORATED WITH WOMEN SERVING WINE AND PLAYING MUSIC

VILLA PAINTER
GREEK
Ceramic
Ashmolean Museum
Oxford, U.K.

Vitis vinifera

century B.C., whose *Works and Days* was the model for Virgil's *Georgics*, wrote of its languid delights:

Then in a great rock's shadow, with milk-bread, let me lie,
And Byblian wine, and milk from goats just going dry,
And flesh of an uncalved heifer, fed in a forest glade,
Or kids first-born of their mother. So let me sit in the shade,
With a bellyful within me, sipping at my ease
The fire-red wine, and turning to face the western breeze.

The Romans—their legionaries in particular—drank gallons of wine, mostly mixed with water. They grew grapes as far afield as southern Britain and upper Egypt. It was no accident that the boundaries of the Roman Empire reflected, more or less, the range of the cultivated grape. River valleys, the vine's natural habitat, of the Rhone, Rhine, Douro, Gironde, and Danube, were the main arterial routes for penetration. In Italy alone there were about eighty cultivars producing red, white and golden wines, sweet and dry, full-bodied or light; wines for keeping or drinking young. Vines were allowed to ramble over walls or trees, or trellises set in lines, and modern rows of vines were unknown.

Wine was stored in pitch-coated jars in the *fumarium*, where the Romans kept wood for winter and smoked hams and cheeses. They loved to dine *al fresco* under vine-covered pergolas, or sleep off a big meal in an outdoor, vine-shaded *diaeta*. Pliny the Younger was proud of the little gazebo in the garden of his Tuscan villa. It had a bed and windows, and "the light inside is dimmed by the dense shade of a flourishing vine which climbs over the whole building up to the roof. There you can lie and imagine you are in a wood but without the risk of rain."

Vine-covered terraces were often fringed by an artificial waterway (*euripus*). The Romans loved sitting in dappled shade and listening to the sound of running water or gazing at the reflection of oil lamps on water at night. To make garlands to wear at banquets or hang around their villas, the Romans made hoops of pliant mulberry or fig, then interwove ivy or vine leaves in season. Vines were a symbol of autumn, and the god of wine and ecstasy was Bacchus (Dionysus in Greece).

There may have been a price to pay, though, for all this carousing. The rich Romans used lead in wine making and in plumbing, painting, cosmetics and cooking (the poor, however, all used earthenware or wineskins). The decline of the imperial ruling cadre, ascribed by Suetonius to gluttony and apathy, is now thought to have been caused by

WALL PAINTING FROM THE TOMB OF MENNA: GRAPE PICKING AND PRESSING, C.1,400 B.C.

(above left)

Chicago Press

U.S.

MOSAIC OF CUPID GATHERING GRAPES

(above)

FOUTH CENTURY A.D.

Naples Museum

Italy

Vitis vinifera   93

León, the boy soldier from Seville who spent seventeen years soldiering in the New World from the 1530s, wrote of vineyards planted in the plains outside Lima. No wine, so far as he was aware, had been made yet and because the vines were irrigated, he feared it would be thin. The Spanish throne offered a bounty of two bars of silver to the first in each settlement to produce four *arrobas* (the equivalent of 100 pounds in liquid weight) of wine, and the same for olive oil.

The first recorded introduction of *vinifera* to the Atlantic coast of North America was in 1621, by the London Company. In 1765 it was transplanted, probably by Jesuit priests, from Mexico to California, where it found a congenial sunny climate that reminded it of home, of the Mediterranean rim; and the same in Chile, where it was being grown as early as 1569. In the southeast of the U.S., and in the Caribbean and even in Venezuela, it hybridized spontaneously with American native species to produce some interesting cultivars.

European vines had historically been pretty much disease-free, but French vines suddenly began to die in 1860 and within a few years there was hardly a vineyard in France unaffected. In 1868 the trouble was traced to a green fly aphid, *Phylloxera vastatrix*, which formed destructive galls on the roots and leaves of the growing plant.

Various remedies were tried: spraying with copper sulphate, even submerging the vines in floodwater. But the long, slow, painful answer proved to be eradication of the vineyards followed by replanting, with European vines grafted onto aphid-resistant American species (*Vitis riparia, rupestris* and *berlandieri* were especially good, mostly from Missouri and the

chronic lead poisoning. Rich Romans under the later empire certainly showed telltale symptoms: anaemia, loss of weight, appetite, and constipation. Their birthrate fell and they died young.

Columbus took vines to plant on his second voyage to the New World in 1493, and soon after the Spanish Conquest, European vines were being grown in Central and South America. In his *Chronicle of Peru*, Cieza de

Midwest). That way the scions retained their ancient vinous characteristics. But grafting is labor-intensive and costly and ever since the first *Phylloxera* outbreak the Holy Grail for vine breeders has been a "French hybrid"—an American x European genotype that combines grape quality with resistance to the devastating insect. The quest to resist phylloxera still continues and varieties with greater hardiness or fungus resistance have turned up en route. One American female vine, Selection 70

(*rupestris x lincecumii*), sent from Missouri to France in 1882, is the genetrix of major wine industries in parts of the world where the European vine does not thrive.

Today, wines are grown around the globe, and New World wines are greatly in favor. But if you are looking for subtlety and grace, it is hard to beat a good wine from the valleys of the Rhone or Gironde, on whose gravels and terraces the Romans planted and cultivated *Vitis vinifera* over 2,000 years ago.

BACCHANAL BEFORE A HERM, C. 1634
NICOLAS POUSSIN
1594–1665
National Gallery
London, U.K.

Citrus fruits Citrus *of the* Rue *family*

The origins of citrus fruits lie in Asia, roughly in the triangle formed by eastern India, Indonesia, and China. When were they domesticated and from which wild ancestors?

Fifty years ago, for evolutionary botanists it was all largely a matter of inspired guesswork. This was greatly the fault of the citrus fruits, as the genera are inexcusably reproductive. Not only do they lustily cross-breed with each other, within genera as well as the species (their hybrids are often sexually fertile too), they are also, in many cases, both self-pollinating and what botanists call "parthenocarpic"—able to produce fruit and fertile seed without sexual mixing.

The results are fairly chaotic, particularly as citrus does not breed true from seed. It is "heterozygous," producing widely diverse seedlings. The only sure way of breeding a selected orange from an orange, or a lime from a lime, is by clonal reproduction: by cuttings of branch or root or, best of all, by grafting the selected scion on to a rootstock.

It is difficult and time consuming to replicate a desired trait, such as resistance to drought, virus or cold, seedlessness, or earlier fruit maturity, in citrus by line breeding. New species—the twentieth-century pink grapefruit is an obvious example—have mostly occurred as chance mutants, sometimes of a single bud or branch on a tree, which have then been fixed (artificially cloned or grafted) by man.

The *Citreae* tribe of the *Rutaceae* family is divided by botanists into twenty-eight genera,

of which six are considered "true" citrus: *Citrus, Fortunella* (the kumquat), *Microcitrus, Eremocitrus, Clymenia,* and *Poncirus.* They are tree-like, vary in size and carry many (up to 200,000) egg-shaped leaves and white or pinkish white flowers. All are evergreen, except *Poncirus,* which loses its leaves in winter and is very resistant to cold. Their range is roughly thirty-five degrees north and south of the equator. All have the typical citrus-smelling oil glands in their peels. One ton of lemon fruit can yield up to 19.8 pounds of essential oil. The color of citrus fruits (they are berries with stalked juice sacs covered with a white spongy tissue called an albedo) depends on yellow, orange, and red pigments called caretonoids. Some of these pigments do not develop unless the temperature drops below 55°F for several hours—which is why tropical oranges hang green on the trees, while, in cooler Mediterranean climes, they are orange or red. Fruits can hang unharvested on trees for up to nine months.

In the 1950s, the Californian botanist W T Swingle subdivided the *Citrus* genus into sixteen species. By the 1970s, it was believed that Swingle's sixteen should be increased to one hundred sixty-two. In the 1990s according to the DNA evidence, the ancestral wild species from which all the commercial citrus fruits derive as hybrids, number only three: the

Citrus

THE BATTLE OF SAN
ROMANO, c.1456
(detail)

PAOLO UCCELLO
*c.*1 3 9 7 – 1 4 7 5
*National Gallery
London, U.K.
Sour oranges, depicted top
left, were the first to arrive
in Europe and represented
wealth, in this case that of
the Medici for whom the
picture was painted*

citron (*Citrus medica*), a lemon-like fruit with a thick, rough peel, but less juicy and lacking the distinctive lemon mammila (nipple) at the non-twig end; the pummelo or shaddock (*Citrus grandis*), still grown and eaten in Asia and resembling a grapefruit and biggest of all the citrus fruits, which the French call *pamplemousse*; and the mandarin or tangerine, (*Citrus reticulata*), which we drop, bagged, into our supermarket shopping carts.

It is tempting to push the story even farther back. The post-war Cambridge botanist E. J. H. Corner argued that the angiosperms, the flowering plants, began their career millions of years ago as tall forest trees in the tropics, and spread out north and south from the equator, getting smaller and shrubbier in their colonizing progress. Is it possible that *Microcitrus*, which grows only in the tropical rainforest of northeastern Australia and has been isolated from other *Citrus* genera for aeons, is the proto-parent? It is a tall, vigorous rain forest tree with small fruit (hence the *Micro*). Could it have engendered the smaller, shrubbier citron or mandarin or pummelo before the continents of Asia and Australia

drifted apart (citrus fruits, like coconuts, cannot survive prolonged immersion in salt water)? Or might it have produced *Eremocitrus glauca*—a small, prostrate, shrubby, drought-resistant plant with greyish-green leaves and typical citrus peel encasing hard, wrinkled seeds—that ekes out a living in the deserts of the Australian outback? It is fun to speculate.

The Chinese were probably the first to domesticate citrus, selecting for their orchards what botanists like to call "superior phenotypes," in perhaps the third or fourth millennium B.C. The earliest documentary evidence for grafting of fruit trees—of citrus trees as it happens—comes from China. Growing fruit trees implies a community settled and self confident enough to justify the necessary investment in the land over ten to fifteen years (corn is fly-by-night, it can be sown and harvested in three months). The Chinese used, as they still do, an intricate system of ditches and berms for irrigation of citrus, or raised their beds above the water table in marshy areas. In winter they sheltered their plants from the cold, just as Italian gardeners today put their citrus pots out when the mulberries come into leaf and bring them in again when autumn frosts threaten. The cliff-defying lemon groves above Amalfi, on the west Italian coast south of Naples, are covered with black plastic netting. Not, as one might imagine, to prevent fruits falling on your head from above, but to insulate the lemon trees below from excessive heat and cold.

From eastern Asia, the culture of citrus moved west—the first Asiatic fruit to do so blazing a trail that would soon be followed by the apricot, quince and peach. Alexander the Great's campaigns in Iran and northern India around 330 B.C. are commonly held to have been responsible for the introduction of the citron, the precursor of the lemon, to the Mediterranean.

Theophrastus (372–287 B.C.), however, pupil of Plato and guardian of Aristotle's children, gives a detailed account of how to grow and propagate citrons, which suggests they were already well known to the Greek world. Citron seeds have also been found at an archaeological site in Cyprus dating from 1,200 B.C., Hala Sultan Tekke, near Larnaka. By Roman imperial times citrons were grown all around the Mediterranean littoral, where they found the climate with warm dry summers and cool wet winters very much to their taste.

Citrons and lemons prefer the sub-tropics; they suffer from blight and virus in excessive tropical heat. The Roman general Lucullus, like Alexander fabulously rich and successful from his Asian campaigns in 60 B.C., is credited with having brought the citron to Italy. The Romans were great plant hunters and experimenters. They seem to have grown it for its timber, medicinal qualities and, above all, for its shady, decorative form, flowers and scent, not, as far as we know, for flavoring food. Pliny the Elder, who called it a Median apple, mentions circular table tops made out of citron wood.

The southern garden of the Villa Poppaea at Oplontis, in the shadow of Vesuvius and buried by the mountain when it erupted in A.D. 79, was planted with two rows of citron trees. Writers of the time, like Columella, a Roman farmer from Cadiz who published a horticultural manual in A.D. 60, were well aware that tender fruits like the citron did well on Mediterranean coasts, but that they needed

OLD DAMASCUS:
JEW'S QUARTER OR
GATHERING
CITRONS, 1873/4
FREDERICK
LEIGHTON
1836–1896
Oil on canvas
Private Collection

protection and fruited later on inland, north facing ground. However, there is not a shred of evidence, in Roman mosaics, wall paintings or literature, for oranges (sweet or sour), lemons, pummelos or mandarins—only for the citron.

The prophet Muhammad died in A.D. 632. Within a century of his death, Islam had swept from Persia through Egypt and North Africa, up into Spain and into the Languedoc; even, later, into parts of Sicily. As the Umayyad Caliphate expanded, vineyards, anathematized by the Prophet, were grubbed out and citrus fruits planted instead. Egypt had been famous in classical times for its delicious wines: never again. This was the cue for oranges, lemons, limes, pummelos and mandarins, probably brought along the east-west sea routes of Arabic commerce to make their first entrance upon the European stage.

The lemon (*Citrus limon*) may have originated in the foothills of the Eastern Himalayas. Wild lemon trees still occur in that area. DNA evidence suggests that the pummelo was its maternal parent, probably crossed with a citron. It likes semi-arid, subtropical regions, where it can flower twice a year, or even all the year round. It does not like the humid tropics. Eureka, which originated in Sicily and was introduced to California in 1858, is the world's favorite cultivar; it has thin smooth peel, and juicy, acidic fruit.

In Renaissance art the lemon is the symbol of fidelity. If you had invited a Roman to "add the zest of a citron" to his food, the chances are that he would not have known what on earth you were talking about. The lemon, say the French, first began to be used in cooking in the reign of Louis XIV in France in the seventeenth

century, when Francois Pierre de la Varenne published three recipe books. La Varenne, who invented puff pastry and popularized truffles, globe artichokes and stuffed mushrooms, hated the heavy meat and almond stews which had dominated French cooking since medieval times. He served vegetables separately and devised piquant sauces made of meat juices combined with vinegar, lemon juice or verjuice (juice of sorrel, sour grapes or crab apples). Europeans of his day were, on the whole, suspicious of fruit: they connected it with summer heat, dysentery and malaria.

Any French claims to have invented cooking with lemons, however, should be taken with a grain of salt. Cultivated Arabs and the Chinese had probably been using them for centuries. They feature in many Dutch and Italian still life paintings from the beginning of the seventeenth century, especially in association with a hunk of bread, fish, lobsters or oysters; often with half their peel spiraling dramatically over the side of the table. In the middle of the seventeenth century you could find good examples to paint in Antwerp. The painter Jan Davidz de Heem moved there in 1636 because "there one could have rarer fruits of all kinds, large plums, peaches, cherries, oranges, lemons, grapes and others, in finer condition and state of ripeness to draw from life."

The lime (*Citrus aurantifolia*), on the other hand, loves the humid tropics. Round with green flesh and a thin, smooth rind, it is the smallest of all the citrus fruits. It hates the cold, and probably originated along the tropical coasts of the Malay archipelago, whence it traveled to India, then across the Gulf of Oman to Arabia and Egypt. The citron, pummelo, and *Microcitrus* are likely to have

played a part in its ancestry.

Introduced to America after the voyages of discovery, it found a congenial home in Mexico (now the world's largest producer of Key limes) and along the Spanish Main. Limes have been grown in the Florida Keys (hence the name) since they were first settled, but a hurricane in 1926 devastated them. There are few trees left now. The largest stand, no bigger than a small apple orchard, is on Islamorada Key. Most American lime juice is extracted from a hybrid lemon, the Tahiti or Bears lime, which originated, despite its name, in America. It is sold green to distinguish it from the true lemon and has bigger leaves and bigger, seedless, less acidic fruit than the Key lime, and purple-petaled flowers (Key lime flowers are white). In the nineteenth century the British Navy used limes, high in vitamin C, to combat scurvy: hence the nickname Limeys.

The sweet orange (*Citrus sinensis*) is the most widely grown citrus fruit in the world. It is eaten fresh, or (mostly) processed into frozen, concentrate orange juice, which was invented in 1948. DNA analysis of germplasm suggests that its parents were the pummelo and mandarin. Like its citrus cousins, it was introduced to the Mediterranean world by the Arabs. In A.D. 976 it is recorded as having been grown in the open by Caliph al-Mansur at Cordoba in southern Spain.

The first Englishmen to come across oranges may well have been crusaders at Jaffa in 1191. This had nothing to do with the naming of Jaffa oranges, which have thick peel, low acidity and good color for the fresh market, and which originated as a bud mutation on a tree near Jaffa, Israel, in 1844.

Marco Polo saw oranges growing north of the straits of Hormuz in Iran at the end of the thirteenth century. He called them "apples of paradise." In 1411, Queen Leonora of Castile grew five orange trees from pips, and in 1499 one of them was sent to Louis XII of France as a wedding present, which suggests they were still regarded as a rare exotic.

They were being grown in Italy from at least the fifteenth century onwards (the Medicis were passionate citrus growers); often in terracotta pots which could be brought into shelter in cold weather. Open plantings were protected by straw, wattle fences and fires. Lord Burghley, who founded the Secret Intelligence Service and for whom spies and plant collectors were more or less out of the same stable, was another keen plant collector. He built a shelter for oranges at Burghley Court in Lincolnshire in 1561, but it is doubtful if they ever fruited: they were probably the sour, Seville oranges used to make marmalade. In 1629, John Parkinson, in his *Paradisi in Sole Paradisus*—the title is a labored pun on his name—recommended growing seedling oranges on hot beds, and picking them when only a few inches high for salads. This gave, he wrote, "a marvellous fine aromaticke or spicy taste, very acceptable."

By the end of the seventeenth century, with the introduction of "stoves" (greenhouses), oranges were being widely grown and fruited in England. In 1690, Sir Francis Carew's gardener at Beddington Park in Surrey boasted a harvest of 10,000 oranges. Today, Brazil is far and away the world's biggest producer. The seedless variety grown worldwide, the

Washingon navel orange, originated as a sweet orange mutant in Bahia, Brazil. It was introduced to Australia in 1824, to Florida in 1835 and to California in 1870.

The sour orange (*Citrus aurantium*) has much the same provenance as sweet orange (pummelo/mandarin/citron parents, southeast Asian origin) and seems to have arrived in the West at the same time. It has been used for centuries as a virus-free rootstock able to withstand wet and dry conditions and its flowers make an oil, Neroli, from which some of the most expensive perfumes are derived. There is evidence that the Chinese were experimenting with citrus-peel oils for perfumes in the third century A.D. In the early 1700s, the bergamot, a sour orange hybrid, became popular in Europe for the same reason.

The mandarin or tangerine (*Citrus reticulata*), one of the three "core" citrus fruits, is believed to have originated in south China or Indo-China. It came late to the West, probably not arriving until maritime trade between Europe and Asia was well developed in late medieval times. The Willowleaf mandarin (*C. deliciosa*), which became the most popular cultivar in the Mediterranean region, did not emerge from China until after 1805, and *reticulata* was introduced to the West even later. It has a short on tree life, so the mandarin season around Christmas used to be a short one. Nowadays the Valencia cultivar extends the fruiting season by carrying two crops simultaneously, mature and immature, on a Californian tree.

The Japanese love mandarins; they supply about half the world's production. The Clementine is a small, seedless cultivar that does very well on the western shores of

Morocco and in Spain, which is the leading producer of citrus around the Mediterranean.

The pummelo (*Citrus grandis*), also called shaddock or pamplemousse, has its area of origin in the south China/India/Malaya region, and grows wild in Fiji. The citrus fruit with the largest leaves, flowers and fruit, it is tolerant of salt and in southeast Asia it can be farmed on coastal marshes reclaimed from the sea. It acquired its name from a ship's captain called Shaddock, employed by the East India Company, who is said to have brought a specimen from Fiji to Barbados in about 1750. It looks like a grapefruit, but there are marked differences. It has a flatter top, is easy to peel and the juice has a sweet, mild flavor.

The grapefruit (*Citrus paradisi*), which Americans, Europeans, and Japanese seem to prefer to the pummelo, is the only citrus fruit of major commercial importance to originate in the New World. Possibly a hybrid and probably a mutant of the pummelo strain that Captain Shaddock brought to the West Indies, it was introduced to Florida, now a major world producer, in 1809 from the Caribbean islands. It likes plenty of heat, and the best grapefruits come from the tropics, or the humid subtropics. Its leaves are smaller than the pummelo's, and its branches more sturdy and spreading, able to support the considerable weights of fruit that hang from them in clusters like grapes (hence the name). Marsh, which is a seedless variety, occurred as a chance seedling in a Florida orchard in the 1860s. Now it is the most widely planted white-fleshed cultivar in the world. The first pink-fleshed grapefruit occurred in 1907, as a mutant limb sport—again in a Florida orchard. Since then, via Hudson (a 1930s bud-sport)

and a dose of radiation by Texas University researchers in the 1950s, Star Ruby was born, with flesh, peel, juice and even its bark a red color.

The kumquat (*Fortunella margarita*) originated in southern China. Uniquely to the *citreae* tribe you can eat it whole, peel included, fresh, candied or even pickled in vinegar. The fruit is small, and looks like an elongated olive. It was placed in the *Fortunella* genus (named after the English plant hunter Robert Fortune) rather than in *Citrus* because of various differences in morphology. It has limited juice and tends to bloom much later in the year than other commercial citrus. The undersides of its leaves have a characteristic silvery color and its habit is vigorous, upright to spreading. The leaves and wood are fairly cold hardy.

It is worth recalling that the early European voyagers to the New World were as much concerned with what they could bring in as with what they could take out. Columbus, on his second voyage to the Americas in 1493, took with him from Gomera in the Canaries seeds of orange, lemon, and citron and planted them in Haiti, where they flourished and spread to other islands in the Caribbean.

In the sixteenth and seventeenth centuries, citrus orchards became well established north and south of the American Land Bridge, spread mostly by Catholic missions. Pedro de Cieza de Léon, who published the first eyewitness account of the conquest of Peru, based on his experiences from 1535 onwards, was fairly indifferent to native plants, but waxed lyrical about the introduced figs, pomegranates, quinces, grapes, and citrus fruits that he had seen growing in the plains around Lima. The home government in Spain offered prizes in the settlements for the first to grow a given

weight of various crops, vegetables, and fruits. It is a pleasant irony that, today, evolutionary botanists go to the *altiplano* of Peru, or the jungles of Ecuador or the Amazon, to research the sources and diversity of plant life. At the beginning of the nineteenth century, citrus was (re)introduced to Australia. If the *Microcitrus* of the Australian rain forest is indeed the proto-parent of citrus, a long circle had at last been closed.

Whither citrus? When conventional breeding techniques are used, hybrids can take up to fifteen years to mature and fruit; the next step can take another five years. Which is why Genetic Modification (GM) and citrus go together well. The Robinson tangerine was not released until 1959, although the original cross between a clementine and tangelo was made in 1942. GM, with its apparent ability to enhance a plant's virtues without importing vices at the same time, enormously quickens the evolutionary process. Take *Poncirus trifoliata* from northern China, for example. The only citrus that is truly deciduous, it can tolerate temperatures down to -9°F and can be grown in the open as far north as Long Island, New York on the 42nd parallel. It can form a stock-proof hedge, because of the long thorns in its leaf axils. But it has one big drawback: ponciridin, a bitter principle that makes its fruit unpalatable so that it has only ever been used for rootstocks.

After the disastrous Florida frosts of 1894 and 1895, there were persistent attempts to introduce its frost hardiness to sweet oranges, but with limited success. Hybridization and back crossing removed most of the bitter taste, but lost the frost-hardiness in the process. GM, however, could soon remove the *Poncirus* frost gene, copy it, and insert it into a sweet orange.

Olive Olea europea *of the* Olive *family*

The olive is a tortoise of a tree: very slow-growing, but long-lived. Some specimens may be among the most ancient trees in the world, perhaps thousands of years old. Living Italian trees, it is claimed, go back to pre-Christian days, to early the Republican era of Ancient Rome.

Olives have been propagated clonally for centuries. They rise again from shoots when their trunks are cut off at ground level, and their cuttings are as easy to strike as willows. If you push thick, yard-long branches (known as truncheons) deep into favorable soil, or lay shorter, slimmer twigs horizontally in a shallow trench, or even cut off and bury the little swellings on the tree trunks (embryonic buds known as *uovoli*), they will soon vegetate and root. Such plants are biologically identical to their parents; contemporary cultivars may well have been grown by Greeks in Classical times. Try growing a sexual generation of cultivated olives from seed and your reward will be, almost invariably, an immediate reversion to the wild genotype, the oleaster olive.

The wild olive (*Olea europea* ssp. *oleaster*), is generally accepted as the ancestor of the cultivated olive. It grows all over the Mediterranean littoral—an exception being the droughty, low-lying coast between eastern Libya and Jordan—wherever the rocky, scrubby *garrigue*, full of herb-like smells, runs down to the wine-dark sea. It likes sea breezes and, particularly, the craggy, limestone shoreline of the Greek peninsula and its adjacent islands.

It is a straggling, evergreen tree, smaller and bushier than its cultivated offspring. It has thorny branches, blunt, gray-green leaves which are dark on top and hoary underneath, small white flowers and smaller fruits, with thinner flesh containing less oil. Cultivated olive groves are often fringed by feral, gone native trees, and it may be difficult to distinguish what has escaped from cultivation from what is truly wild: the oleaster olive, in other words, in its drift eastwards from the Levant along the north and south coasts of the Mediterranean, is very likely to have thumbed a lift from human cultivation.

It will stand some frost, but loathes the tropics—climatologists can define a Mediterranean climate by where wild olives grow. Other *Olea* species (there are thirty-five to forty in the genus) grow in tropical, eastern and southern Africa, in southern Arabia, southern Iran and Afghanistan, and in south Asia and eastern Australia, but none of them are thought to have played a part in the evolution of the cultivated olive. One rather similar species (*O. laperrinei*), that grows in isolation in the Atlas mountains of the Sahara, is possibly an ancient genetic bridge between the oleaster olives of the Mediterranean and the more tropical loving trees of the African

And the dove came in to him in the evening; and, lo, in her mouth was an olive leaf pluckt off; so Noah knew that the waters were abated from off the earth.

Genesis 8:11

DOVE, 1961
PABLO PICASSO
1881–1973
Pastel on paper
Private Collection

MAN PLANTING
OLIVES AND A
HOUND
(detail)
THE NEPTUNE
MOSAIC
Bardo Museum
Tunis, Tunisia

savannah—though whether *Olea* moved north or south, at the time, remains a mystery.

Olives were probably collected in the wild by hunter-gatherers in the Levant long before their cultivation. They are inedible straight off the tree, and need to be soaked in a salt solution to reduce their bitter taste. The oil, however, can be expressed straight from the fruit by a simple process of crushing and squeezing. Early man may have hit upon eating fresh olives by picking up fallen fruits on the Mediterranean shore.

It is well nigh impossible for archaeologists to distinguish between stones of wild and cultivated trees without other supporting evidence. The earliest known human collection of olive stones, in deposits from 9,000–8,000 B.C. in the Mount Carmel area in Israel, is assumed to be from wild fruit.

The first evidence of olive cultivation comes from Tuleilat Ghassul, at levels equivalent to the fourth millennium B.C. Here, north of the Dead Sea in the Jordan valley, carbonized olive stones and pieces of charred olive wood have been found in an area too dry for the wild olive and some way outside its present day range. An educated guess is that the Tuleilat Ghassul olives were artificially selected, planted, and irrigated by humans, just as they are today in the Jordan valley, and that the olive was brought into cultivation somewhere along the southwestern coast of the Levant in the first tranche of fruits—the date palm, olive, grapevine, and fig—in the millennia that followed the invention of grain farming in the Middle East, some 10,000 years ago. Other sites near Tuleilat Ghassul have yielded masses of crushed olive stones, which suggest that olive presses were already at work by about 3,500 B.C.

Outside Israel and Palestine, evidence of human olive use is much later: in Syria in the 3rd millennium BC and in Crete in the second, by which date olive culture and olive oil production were well established in the southern Levant, with a thriving, well documented export trade from Palestine to Egypt (the plant has never liked the rich, alluvial soils and hot, dry climates of Egypt and Mesopotamia). By about 1,000 B.C. cultivation began in mainland Greece and the islands. Presses and olive oil pots have been found throughout the Aegean, and olive motifs start to feature in Greek Bronze Age art.

In the succeeding centuries, Greek and Phoenician colonists sailed to the western end of the Mediterranean and planted olives along the coasts of North Africa, Italy, Sicily, and Spain. They may have ventured out into the Atlantic as far as Madeira and the Canaries, where ancient olive trees are said to have greeted the medieval rediscoverers of the islands, and a plant given separate subspecies status—*O. europea* var. *maderiensis*—now contentedly grows in the wild.

To Greeks of the Homeric period, about 1,000 B.C., olive oil was an imported luxury, a toiletry of the very rich. Heroes in the *Iliad* anointed their bodies with it after a bath, and the corpse of Patroclus, bosom friend of Achilles, was sprinkled with olive oil at his funeral. The olive gets several mentions in the *Odyssey*, but only in rather idealized contexts, like the description of the fabulous gardens of Alcinous, king of the Phaeacians; Homer, otherwise keen on gardening, seems ignorant of its culture. But 400 years later, in classical times, olive growing was commonplace throughout Greece and the islands—the playwright Aeschylus in his *Persae*, produced in Athens in 472 B.C., called Samos *elaiophutos* "planted with olives."

Olive oil off the Attica limestone was reputed to be the best in the world: its export made Athens rich. It was the city's sacred tree and grew by the goddess Athene's hand straight out of solid rock on the Acropolis and sprouted again from the root when the tree's trunk was destroyed during the Persian wars. Her citizens used olive oil for cooking and eating. It provided a butter substitute for their bread, oil for their lamps and soap for their baths. They soaked green olives in "lye," a solution of alkaline salts made from wood ashes soaked in water, then pickled them in brine and ate them whole, spitting out the pips, just as we do today.

From earliest times, olives symbolized peace, victory, wealth and prosperity; a gift of a tree or of an olive

OLIVE OILS

St Andrew and St
Jerome

Jacopo Robusti
Tintoretto
1518–1594
*Galleria dell'Accademia
Venice, Italy*

branch was a pacific even submissive gesture. The Egyptians, who called the olive *tat*, put leaves and branches in the sarcophagi of their wealthy dead. Olive branches were carried in the Greater Panathenaea—the festival held once every four years at Athens and celebrated in the British Museum's Parthenon frieze. Victors in the Olympic games wore wild olive sprays.

Pliny the Elder, who wrote a thirty-seven-volume book, *Naturalis Historia,* and died in the Bay of Naples when his ship was overwhelmed by the eruption of Vesuvius in A.D. 79, recorded that no olive trees existed in Italy in the reign of Tarquinius Pristus in the seventh century B.C. He was wrong: they had long since arrived with Greek settlers.

In the later days of the Republic, Italy was exporting olive oil to her provinces in northern Europe, and her citizens were fond of reminding you that the secret of a long and happy life was "wine within, and oil without." Pliny described fifteen different cultivars. The best oil, he said, came from the Naples region. To make scents, the Romans boiled down fragrant parts of plants, such as the flowers, roots or leaves (attar of Turkish damask rose petals was popular) and mixed them with olive oil to smear on their bodies.

The excavation of the ancient port of Pisa, discovered by a bulldozer in December 1998, beneath the intended site of a new railway station, has revealed more than ten Roman ships preserved in river mud. One of them was a cargo ship with stacked, sealed jars, containing the remains of whole olives. Other jars were filled with peaches, walnuts, cherries, plums, wine and, oddly, sand (probably used as a degreasing agent in making pottery). The amphoras were propped up with bricks of Vesuvian lava, and archaeologists today believe that the ship had sailed up the coast from the Bay of Naples and was unloading at Pisa when it was overwhelmed by a flash flood, which descended from the Luccan hills.

After the discovery of the New World, Spanish settlers took the olive tree to the

Pacific coast of South America, where it grew well in the lee of the Andes. The story of its introduction to Chile and Peru is told by Garcilaso de la Vega in his *Commentarios Reales*, published in Lisbon in 1609. In 1560, a Spanish neighbor of his in Peru, Don Antonio de Ribera, brought two pots containing one hundred olive cuttings from Seville. Only three plants survived the voyage. They were planted in the Spaniard's walled fruit farm near Cuidad de los Reyes and guarded night and day by one hundred Indians and thirty dogs. But one plant was stolen from under their noses and reappeared within a few days, miles away in Chile "where it produced offspring so successfully for that kingdom during the next three years that they did not plant a cutting, no matter how scrawny, that didn't take root and quickly turn into a handsome olive tree."

In the seventeenth century, Jesuit missionaries introduced the tree to Mexico and upper California, and Australian planters in the nineteenth century found it did very well in Queensland and in South Australia near Adelaide. Today, countries of the Mediterranean basin—Spain, Turkey, Italy, Greece and Tunisia—are still the world's leading producers of olives and olive oil, but California, Mexico and Chile, Australia and South Africa, are not far behind.

THE OLIVE PICKERS, SAINT-REMY, 1889
VINCENT VAN GOGH
1853–1890
Private Collection

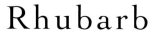

Rhubarb

Rheum rhabarbarum *of the* Dock *family*

Rhubarb is a plant of parts—and you need to be sure which part you are eating. Its dried and powdered root has been used in medicine for thousands of years and is highly effective in emptying the digestive system, bugs and all. Doctors in the tropics have attested its almost miraculous powers in treating, for instance, amoebic dysentery.

In the late eighteenth century, when sugar became cheaper in Europe, rhubarb's tart, young stems began to be cooked and eaten by Westerners as a vegetable (or, if you follow the 1947 U.S. Customs ruling, as a fruit). The leaves, however, cooked or uncooked, contain enough oxalic acid to kill when ingested. A verdict in an English coroner's court in 1901, read "Accidental death, caused by eating rhubarb-leaves." In a case in the 1920s, rhubarb leaves were carefully washed, drained, cut up, then boiled in water for twenty minutes in an iron saucepan and served like spinach. They proved to be lethal.

The rhubarb or *Rheum* genus, related to docks and sorrels, includes about twenty wild perennial species, high altitude plants that range from the mountains of Turkey and the Caucasus, via the Pamirs and Himalayas to central China and up into Siberia. They enjoy harsh winters. Their rhizomatous roots lie dormant beneath the snow, then grow rapidly in early springtime.

R. rhabarbarum, the principal wild parent of our garden rhubarb, is found in an arc from the Tien Shan mountains in central Asia through Mongolia to western China.

Two similar species, but with inedible stems, *R. officinalis* and *R. palmatum*, (the latter with deeply-lobed leaves) originate in the mountains of eastern Asia and are widely cultivated in China for anthaquinone, the purgative drug in their roots. Traditionally, they were sliced crossways, hung up to dry in the sun with string through a hole in their middles, then ground into powder. The roots of *rhabarbarum*, or garden rhubarb, also contain the drug, but not in such quantities.

The first references to rhubarb occur in the Chinese *Pen-King* herbal, dated to 2,700 B.C. Though doubts have been expressed about the herbal's authenticity, it is fairly certain that the root was being used in Chinese medicine by 200 B.C., and probably long before that.

Dioscorides was a Roman army doctor from Cilicia (southeast Turkey), who compiled a pharmaceutical list of about five hundred herbs in the first century A.D. One of them was a root he called in Greek *rheon* or *rha*, which he said came from beyond the Bosphorus.

Dioscorides' *rheon* is thought to be the same as the Latin *Rheum barbarum*, an exotic root connected by the Romans of the later empire with the river Volga and apparently used by them as a purgative. There is no reference to rhubarb by any of the Roman gardening authors, so one assumes they imported the dried or powdered root to Italy, rather than growing it on the Mediterranean rim. This would make sense, particularly as rhubarb also dislikes hot, sea-level habitats. With the decline of the Roman Empire, the use of rhubarb root seems to have been forgotten, in Europe at least, for many centuries.

By Marco Polo's day, at the end of the thirteenth century, however, there was a

STILL LIFE WITH RHUBARB, *c.*1930
ARCHIBALD McGLASHAN
Oil on canvas
Berwick upon Tweed
Borough Museum and
Art Gallery, U.K.

renewed interest in the plant. Polo wrote that it grew "in great abundance" in the mountains of northwest China:

It is bought here by merchants, who export it far and wide.

A century after Polo's travels, so-called "East Indian Rhubarb-root" was reaching Europe by the Arab sea route that brought other spices like black pepper, cinnamon and ginger, via the Persian Gulf and Red Sea to Alexandria; Turkey rhubarb came in overland on the Silk Road from Persia and the Caspian Sea to the Mediterranean ports of Aleppo and Smyrna.

Because of the long distances traveled, and the danger of loss by bug attack, the drug commanded huge prices in Europe—in 1542 it was sold in France for ten times the price of cinnamon and an English price list from 1657 quoted rhubarb at sixteen shillings per pound, more than double than that of opium at six shillings. The powder had two, paradoxical uses: in small doses, up to two grains, as an astringent, "binding" tonic; in large doses, fifteen to thirty grains, as a crash purgative.

In 1614, Giacomo Castelvetro, an Italian exile in England, recommended chewing through an ounce of raisins, previously soaked in dry, not sweet, malmsey wine, then sieve-dried and mixed with a dram of powdered rhubarb, as a cure for constipation. For over forty years, he wrote, he had used this recipe successfully on himself and his friends. three hundred years later, in 1921, Dr. Burkitt reported in *The Lancet* that he had routinely treated cases of acute dysentery in the British colony of Kenya with powdered rhubarb, thirty grains every two or three hours until the rhubarb appeared in the stools:

After a few doses the stools become less frequent, haemorrhage ceases, and straining and the other symptoms of acute general poisoning, which characterise the disease, rapidly disappear...I know of no remedy in medicine which has such a magical effect.

In 1653, China opened up her borders to trade with Russia, who, in the eighteenth century, established a virtual monopoly of the rhubarb trade to Europe. High-quality "Russian" rhubarb was imported via the border town of Kiachta in Siberia, where Russian government inspectors bored little holes in each piece of root to make sure it was properly dried and up to standard. By the nineteenth century, however, with Chinese coastal ports open to European trade, growers in China were mass-producing roots of inferior standard in response to increased demand, and by about 1860 the market in Europe for quality "Russian" rhubarb had more or less collapsed.

Early attempts to make a fortune by growing medicinal rhubarb in Europe met with mixed success, for the Chinese guarded the culture and processing of *officinale* and *palmatum* as jealously as their manufacture of the roots of *rhaponticum* contain less anthaquinone than the Chinese species, and although prizes were distributed by the English Society of Arts in the later eighteenth century for growing rhubarb roots—a Banbury apothecary called Hayward won their gold medal in 1794—the English rhubarb trade, which at one time exported to America, was always at a disadvantage.

Rhaponticum, though, has edible stems like *rhabarbarum*—indeed, the two species are now considered synonymous—and it was not long before Europeans realized they could make a meal from this delicious plant.

The English naturalist John Ray noted in his *Historia Plantarum* (1686) that rhubarb stalks were as good to eat as those of sorrel; one Peter Collinson noted in a letter to a friend in September 1739 that what he called "Siberian rhubarb," peeled and baked in a pie with sugar and cinnamon:

has none of the effects that the roots have. It eats most like gooseberry pie.

As sugar became cheaper and more available in Europe and North America at the end of the eighteenth century, so the tart stems of cooked rhubarb featured more and more in the repertoire of cooking in the West and classic Victorian puddings like rhubarb and custard and rhubarb crumble were conceived.

In North America, where introduced rhubarb proved to be very popular, it soon became known as the Pie plant.

In 1815, it was discovered at the Chelsea Physic Garden, apparently by accident, that when cultivating rhubarb one could force it in

RHUBARB, 1905
J. STURMS
Etching from Flora von
Deutschland *by*
H.L. Krause
Stuttgart, Germany

silk in Roman and Byzantine times. Prosper Alpinus got hold of seed of *R. rhaponticum* from central Asia, and grew it at Padua's Botanic Garden at the beginning of the seventeenth century, and seeds of it are said to have been brought to England from Italy by Charles I's doctor and given to the botanist Parkinson. But

Rheum rhabarbarum

early spring to produce long, tender shoots by covering the crowns with a pot. At about the same time, nurserymen like Hawkes of Lewisham and Joseph Myatt of Deptford were experimenting with hybrids of rhubarb species to produce cultivars of varying earliness, acidity and color. Hawkes' Champagne, a still popular variety from the early nineteenth century, has stalks that are slim, sweet, early and red at the base.

The Poles still cook rhubarb as a tart, vegetable accompaniment to potatoes, and in Iran it is put into stews. The Italians use it for a low alchohol aperitif, known as *rabarbaro*.

CABBAGE AND RHUBARB

MARK GERTLER

1891–1939

Connaught Brown

London, U.K.

Banana   Musa cultivars *of the* Banana *family*

Edible bananas first grew in southeast Asia, probably in the Malaysian peninsula, tens of thousands of years ago. They are primitive plants, in construction not far removed from the first trees of the primeval forest. They may have been one of the earliest fruits to have been brought into cultivation by man.

We know from archaeological evidence of preserved cereal grains and fruit seeds that the river lands between the Nile and the Indus—the so-called Fertile Crescent— were being farmed in Mesolithic times (c. 8,000 B.C.). But it has also been argued that primitive hunter gatherers, living along the coastlines of southeast Asia, supplemented their protein-rich fish diets by planting corms of starchy bananas and tubers of root crops, and knew the art of clonal propagation many thousands of years before Middle East farmers sowed their first cereal seeds. Malaysian banana growers, in other words, may have been the world's first farmers. Hard evidence, however, is elusive: edible bananas are seedless, and leave no archaeological trace in human coprolites (fossilised dung). Early tuber crops would have been equally perishable, compared to the cereals and nuts of the Middle East. The prehistory of southeast Asia remains largely a matter of guesswork.

Bananas are easy enough to grow, given the right conditions. They are large (6.6–19.8ft high), herbaceous perennial herbs that put out suckers or stools from a central stump. They like the wet tropics or the drier subtropics and hate frost, bad drainage and high winds: thirty-five degrees north and south of the equator is about as much as they can manage.

A time-honored way of growing them is to hack back the bush, or clear the jungle canopy, and plant the corms with minimal cultivation amid the rotting vegetation. The corm grows what appears to be a stem but is in fact about thirty tightly clasping leaf sheaths, like a cigar; the true stem pushes up the "cigar's" middle and produces female flowers which, unpollinated, become banana bunches or "hands" with "fingers" (the bananas). The leaves are vast and spreading, and filled with a milky juice; they wilt in prolonged sunshine, and stiffen up again at night. Ecuador and Guinea, two of the world's leading producers, are overcast for much of the year.

About forty species of the *Musa* genus have been identified by botanists growing wild in southeast Asia and the Pacific islands, and there are probably more still undiscovered. Almost all have seedy, fairly inedible fruits and are of little practical use. Leaf fibres of *Musa textilis,* which grows in Borneo and the Philippines, have been used to make ship's ropes. The edible when cooked Fe'i banana, which originated in the New Guinea/Solomon Islands area and was dispersed by man across

and sterile (the fruit was seedless and therefore edible). In technobotanical terms, it changed from a diploid plant (with two chromosome chains and able to pollinate) into a triploid (three chromosome chains—an uneven number, so unable to pollinate). Humans ate it, liked it and took it into cultivation. They migrated northwest with it, towards India and the cold, cooler monsoon climate. There, it hybridized with an inedible wild seedy banana, *balbisiana*, whose genes lent it some resistance to drought and cold and the ability to survive in cooler, subtropical conditions. The ancestral clone of the banana cultivar, of which there are about three hundred that we know today, was created.

The first mention of plants identifiable as bananas comes from India, in the Buddhist literature of the sixth century B.C. There is no trace of them in ancient Chinese texts, but that is not so surprising: Chinese culture evolved in cooler, northern latitudes, well away from the banana growing tropics.

Bananas were known to the Mediterranean, classical world only by repute. Alexander the Great had come across them on his Indian campaigns either side of 330 B.C.; or so claimed his contemporary Theophrastus, who succeeded Aristotle as principal of the Peripatetic School at Athens. Pliny the Elder finished his massive thirty-seven-volume book *Naturalis Historia* in A.D. 77, two years before he died on his ship in the Bay of Naples when Vesuvius erupted. Pliny said that the fruit that Alexander had seen was eaten by Indian wise men. Seventeen centuries later, Linnaeus, who knew his Pliny, christened the banana *Musa sapientium*: incorrectly, as it turned out, for the banana Linnaeus was describing was a hybrid

the Pacific, has erect bunches and red juice. In Tahiti it is cut down by hunters in the hill-forests and carried down to market on poles. The Tahitians never eat it fresh. They used to roast it in pits; now they boil or steam it.

One wild species native to the Malay peninsula, *M. acuminata*, acquired two characteristics by mutation many millennia ago: it became both parthenocarpic (able to make large, pulpy fruit without pollination)

cultivar, not a wild species.

The prophet Muhammad died in 632. Within a century of his death, Islam had swept from Persia through Egypt and North Africa, up into Spain and into the Languedoc; even, later, into parts of Sicily. As the Umayyad Caliphate expanded, rooting out vines which the prophet abhorred and planting oranges and lemons in their place, it brought in its wake knowledge of the banana, which the Arabs called *Mouz* or *Moz* (hence the generic name *Musa*, given to it by Linnaeus—did he know Arabic too?). This is the Koran's Tree of Paradise, just as the unnamed tree in the Garden of Eden, perhaps a fig, is the Bible's Tree of Knowledge.

Whether the banana was ever eaten in Europe before the Renaissance must be very doubtful. The problem was one of transport and perishability: Africa north of the Sahara is outside the banana's comfortable range and the nearest major exporting country would have been India's Malabar coast—weeks, if not months, away by Arab dhow and caravan.

The first certain evidence of banana growing in Africa comes from Mombasa in Kenya in A.D. 1300. The banana's route thither was either via Arabia and Ethiopia or, more likely, corms of bananas sailed with Indonesians across the Indian Ocean to Madagascar during the first millennium A.D. They migrated north up the great lakes to Kenya, turned left across the damp heart of Africa and arrived on the West African coastline in time to greet the European explorers of the fourteenth century, who called them "Banemas" or "Banamas" (*sic*), the name given to them by the tribesmen of Guinea.

They were grown in the Canary Islands some time after 1402, when an expedition backed by the Spanish kingdom of Castile finally subdued the Guanches islanders. From there, Tomas de Berlanga, a Dominican friar, introduced bananas to Santo Domingo in the Dominican Republic in 1516, whence they spread south across the Caribbean to colonise the Spanish Main. Some say they were there already in the New World, having come round the other way from Malaysia. There is no doubt that they island hopped with Polynesians in their migration east across the Pacific and probably did so as early as the first millennium A.D. But whether they made the jump to the Americas is unlikely; hard evidence for pre-Columbian bananas in the New World is more or less nonexistent.

MOSAIC OF THE TREE OF PARADISE (*detail*)
UMAYYAD MOSQUE
DAMASCUS, SYRIA
A 1960s reconstruction of the original Umayyad Koranic vision of Paradise

When did they become common fare in the northern hemisphere? Sixteenth- and early seventeenth-century painters of fruit stalls and still lifes, amid a cornucopia of other exotic fruit, never seem to feature bananas.

In 1573 Leonhardt Rauwulf, a German doctor, traveled from Augsburg to North Africa to try and see for himself the strange herbs mentioned by classical writers like Dioscorides. In Tripoli he recorded seeing a banana hitherto unknown in Germany; he was also attacked by a crowd of Muslims at the city's gates and had to run for cover to the Fondique, a warehouse protected by the French consul.

It was always thought that the first bananas ever seen in Britain were imported from Bermuda and hung up to ripen in his shop window in 1633 by Thomas Johnson, a herbalist and royalist near London's Fleet Street who later died in the Civil War. "Some have judged it to be the forbidden fruit," claimed Johnson modestly.

It was with huge excitement then, in the early summer of 1999, that archaeologists from the Museum of London, excavating in the Southwark area, found a blackened but well-preserved banana skin (6in long), that was dateable by the level at which it was found to A.D. 1500. Where had it come from and how? Did bananas feature in Tudor English fruit bowls? Almost certainly not. Fresh fruit was regarded with great suspicion in those days as it was connected with late summer heat, dysentery and the ague—now known as malaria—which was at that time widespread in northern Europe. So, the Southwark banana was most probably a curiosity imported from West Africa.

It was not until the nineteenth century that the world's banana trade, today exceeded only by that of citrus, really took off. Fast schooners—banana boats—raced each other from the Caribbean to Liverpool and from Brazil to New York, straining to deliver their valuable cargo on time. Nineteenth-century bananas in a northern hemisphere fruit bowl, were, like pineapples, a mark of wealth and taste.

Steamships boosted the banana trade and in 1899 the United Fruit Company was set up in Boston. Its Great White Fleet was the first to use chilled holds in its ships (in 1901). With the money it made from bananas it built railways and financed governments and ran the banana republics of Central and Southern America as personal fiefdoms for decades.

The leading cultivar at the beginning of the nineteenth century, Gros Michel, was largely wiped out by Panama disease or banana wilt, which makes the plant smell strongly of rotten fish. Now one of the world's most widely planted cultivars is Dwarf Cavendish, which originated in the Chatsworth greenhouses of the Duke of Devonshire in 1836—it likes the subtropics and does very well in the Canary Islands.

Vegetables

"I saw an old man, a Corycian, who owned a few poor acres of land once derelict, useless for arable, no good for grazing, unfit for the cultivation of vines. But he laid out a kitchen garden in rows amid the brushwood, bordering it with white lilies, verbena, small-seeded poppy. He was happy there as a king. He could go indoors at night to a table heaped with dainties he never had to buy."

GEORGICS IV 130 FF, by Publius Virgilius Maro, pastoral and epic poet of Rome.
Virgil died in 19 B.C., aged 51. He was buried at Naples.

ALLEGORY OF SUMMER (detail)
LUCAS VAN VALCKENBORCH
1535–1597
Oil on canvas
Johnny van Haeften
Gallery, London, U.K.

Pea

Pisum sativum *of the* Pea *family*

The pea was one of the earliest domesticated plants in the Old World. At first gathered, it was selected and improved under cultivation in the Middle Eastern arc, from Turkey to the Caspian Sea.

Nikolai Vavilov, the Soviet botanist and geneticist who scoured the world between the First and Second World Wars for new plants to feed the Russian Revolutionaries, and later disappeared into Stalin's Gulag, identified three possible centers of origin for the wild pea genus: Ethiopia, the Mediterranean, and central Asia. Asia is perhaps the likeliest bet.

The genus consists of two, self-pollinating annual species: *Pisum fulvum*, local to the eastern Mediterranean, with distinctive yellow-brown flowers; and *Pisum sativum*, which ranges right round the Mediterranean rim and on into central Asia, and which botanists have subdivided into ssp. *elatius* and *humile*. *Elatius* is the taller, coastal, western type, and its blue-green foliage and rosy red flowers can be seen sprawling through the Mediterranean's maquis thickets from April to June. *Humile* grows in the Middle Eastern arc from the Levant to the Caucasus. It is shorter, has smaller flowers, and is moretolerant to drought, and is equally at home in the sparse, deciduous oak woodland or open steppes of the region, whence it often spills out as a weed into cultivated land. This subspecies, similar to some cultivated forms except that its seed coats tend to be rough and tough for survival, its seeds slightly bitter, and its pods to shatter early for optimum seed dispersal, is believed to be the progenitor of all the many hundreds of pea varieties that we grow today in our fields and gardens. It hybridizes readily with *elatius* and where the two, wild subspecies rub shoulders on the eastern Mediterranean rim, there is a certain amount of morphological blurring between the two.

The common pea, of course, was the plant that the nineteenth-century Czech (at that time Moravian) monk, Gregor Mendel, used for his experiments that founded the science of genetics. Mendel demonstrated that by hybridizing tall peas with dwarfs, or purple-flowered peas with whites, he could predict that, by the third generation, what he called the "dominant" gene (in the pea's case, tallness and purple flowers) would outbid the "recessive" gene (dwarfness and whiteness) by a fixed ratio. Twentieth-century cytology has since confirmed Mendel's experiments.

Charred pea seeds have been recovered from early Neolithic farming villages in the near East, such as Çayönü in southeast Turkey (7,500–7,000 B.C.). The fragments of rough seed coats suggest that they were gathered, or

1.

1.

2.

3.

3.

4.

5.

6.

Ad. nat. pict. in horto. Benary.

Chromolith. G. Severeyns. Bruxelles.

ERNST BENARY, ERFURT.

PLATE III.—THE RESULT OF CROSSING A YELLOW WRINKLED
WITH A GREEN ROUND PEA

(Top left) Yellow Wrinkled Parent.   (Top right) Round Parent.
(Five Peas in middle line) First Hybrid Generation.

**THE RESULT OF
CROSSING A YELLOW
WRINKLED PEA WITH
A GREEN ROUND PEA**

*Heritable characteristics
researched by Gregor
Mendel*

Once domesticated, the common pea, with its high protein content, ease of culture and long storage life when dried, quickly became a crop staple for early farmers. One can trace the expansion of Stone Age farming in Europe, Africa and Asia by the carbonized remains of smooth coated seeds: Nea Nikomedia in Greece, *c.*5,500 B.C.; Merimde in the Nile Delta *c.*5,000 B.C.; Tell Azmak in Bulgaria, *c.*4,330 B.C.; the Lower Rhine Valley *c.*4,300 B.C.; the western Mediterranean basin and India's Gangetic plain, *c.*2,000 B.C. In China, the earliest evidence for their arrival dates from the Tang dynasty, in A.D. 618–906.

The Greeks grew and ate peas, which they called *pisoi* (the Latin name is *pisum*). Schliemann found a large pot at Hissarlik, the site of Homeric Troy, containing more than 440 pounds of peas, and entertained visitors with peas for dinner "from Priam's larder." Theophrastus, pupil of Plato and friend of Aristotle, mentions peas in his fourth-century-B.C. *History of Plants* and according to Pliny the Elder, writing in the first century A.D., the noble Roman family of Piso derived its name from cultivating the pea. It is also likely that the Romans, who were great plant transferrers throughout their empire, introduced the pea to Britain, like many other vegetables and fruits.

No Greek or Roman writer has left a detailed description of any particular pea variety and it was not until the sixteenth century that a distinction began to be made between varieties of "field" peas, with colored flowers and small pods, and "garden" peas with mainly white flowers and bigger seeds. Before about 1550, on the evidence of medieval monastic accounts, it was mainly field peas that were grown—harvested ripe and stored over

from weedy peas in the fields of corn. Farther west in Turkey, the important Neolithic town of Çatal Hüyük, dating back to 6,500 B.C., was excavated during the 1960s. The pre-ceramic inhabitants boiled cooking water in wooden pots by inserting hot stones from a fire, and ate hybrid and smooth-coated peas. Here, from levels dated *c.*5,750 B.C., are the signs that the wild pea was being deliberately selected and improved under cultivation.

the winter. The dry peas were ground into a flour with rye or wheat and made into bread, or, when needed, soaked overnight and used for pease porridge (often eaten with salted bacon) or pease pudding, or even, like faba beans, used for animal fodder. In Scotland, pea flour—peasemeal—mixed with water, milk or whey, was baked on a griddle to make "bannocks," a common food for the poor.

The practice of eating peas green and immature—the frozen peas we buy at the supermarket are simply peas picked unripe; French *petit pois* are ordinary pea cultivars picked very unripe—seems to have been unknown, at least until well after the Renaissance. At the end of the seventeenth century Madame de Maintenon recorded the latest craze of the court ladies of Louis XIV: eating green peas at all hours of the day, even before they went to bed. "*C'est une mode, un fureur,*" she wrote to a correspondent. Never in the Scottish Border Country, though, where they still like their peas mushy: canned, and treated with alkali to make them starchy.

Thomas Hill, whose *Gardener's Labyrinth* was published in 1577, recommended successional sowings of what he called "the great Rounseval pease," in February, March and April. This may have been a tall, large-seeded, "marrow fat" type of pea, the name having been taken from Roncesvaulx Abbey in Navarre via the Hospital of St Mary Ronceval; "Rounseval pease" are thought to have been cultivated in both places.

Thomas Knight, a Herefordshire cider maker who became president of the Horticultural Society experimented with wrinkled pea crosses in 1787 and commercialized cultivars that were sweeter and more palatable. Knight's wrinkled peas contained more sugar and less starch. His experiments were intended to demonstrate how cider apples could be improved and were the first recorded attempt in history to produce new varieties of a crop under controlled conditions. He anticipated Gregor Mendel by about seventy years, but overlooked the world-changing genetic implications of the Czech monk's work.

At the turn of the twentieth century canned peas proved popular with consumers from the West, but the heat of the canning process destroyed the chlorophyll, turning them a drab, khaki color—greenness could only be introduced with a dye. So when frozen peas, which keep their color, arrived in the 1920s they were an immediate hit. Today, immature peas that are frozen as soon as they are harvested, are a world-wide household convenience food and are about the freshest peas that money can buy.

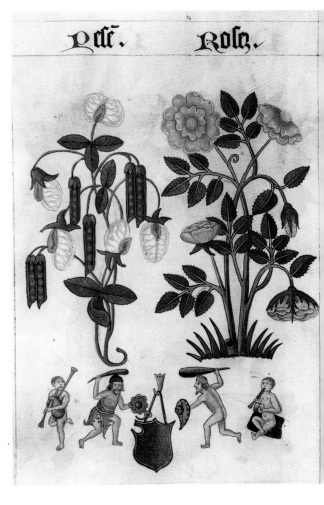

PEAS AND ROSES FROM A TUDOR PATTERN BOOK, 1504
Bodleian Library Collection Oxford, U.K.

Beans

Vicia faba *and* Phaseolus *of the* Pea *family*

The *faba* bean—also called field, winter, tick, horse or broad bean—has been cultivated in the Old World since at least biblical times. It is an easy-to-grow annual with large, nutritious, leguminous, protein-rich seeds that still constitute an important part of the diet of the world's poor.

STILL LIFE WITH
BROAD BEAN PODS

(opposite)

GIOVANNA GARZONI

1600–1670

Oil on parchment

Galleria Palatina

Florence, Italy

Subsistence farmers like the bean because it shrugs off northern frosts or Mediterranean heat and stands up to wind and rain; its root nodules also feed nitrogen from the air back into the soil. In Egypt or Syria the bean crop is planted in December, flowers in the third week of February, and is harvested at the end of June. In northern Europe, once sown in November, it will be ready to eat (if the winter seedlings have not been attacked by slugs and snails) before Midsummer's Day. Easily shucked, the seeds can be eaten fresh or dried, or mixed with grain flour to make bread, or used as fodder for cattle and horses. Camels greatly enjoy chewing at the stalks.

Modern botanists have found no equivalent plant to the broad bean in the wild, which raises the question: from what plant did it originate and when? Alphonse de Candolle, in his *Origines des Plantes Cultivées* of 1882, wrote of an eighteenth-century Russian traveler called Lerche who found *faba* flowering in the Mungan desert of the Mazanderan to the south of the Caspian Sea and gave a specimen to the herbarium of the Imperial Garden at St Petersburg. Lerche's bean resembled cultivated

Vicia faba in every respect, except it was only 6 inches high. Since then, no trace has been found in the Mungan desert or anywhere else. The wild progenitor of *faba* may, in fact, have long been extinct.

The nearest wild equivalent of the broad bean is probably *Vicia narbonensis*, a slender vetch-like plant with long purple flowers, downy black seed pods and a Mediterranean basin range. But its chromosome number (2n=14) is different from *faba* (2n=12) and that, in genetic terms, is a Berlin Wall: all attempts to hybridize the two species have failed.

Both beans, however, may derive from a common, extinct ancestor. Subsistence famers have long been in the habit of allowing *narbonensis* beans to grow as edible weeds among their cereals and to harvest the two together and it is not always easy for archaeologists to tell the seeds of the two species apart. Early *faba* beans were small (no bigger than ¼in), about the size of a modern *petit pois*. But a hoard of 2,600 well-preserved, charred, distinctively flat seeds, that were excavated at a Stone Age settlement near Nazareth in Israel, were almost certainly

Samuel II: 17, 27–29

And it came to pass, when David was come to Mahanaim, that
Shobi . . . and Machi . . . brought wheat and parched corn, and
beans . . . for the people that were with him, to eat: for they said,
The People is hungry, and weary, and thirsty, in the wilderness.

cultivated *fabas*. They date from about 6,500
B.C. and are the earliest known. Other beans
have turned up at sites in Syria and Cyprus, but
they are more globular and like *narbonensis* and
may well have been gathered from the wild.

By the third millennium B.C., rather larger
faba beans (¼–½in) that must have been selected
and improved under cultivation, begin
occurring at sites as far apart as Spain, Portugal,
Greece, the Levant—and in central Europe
too, as far north as Germany and well outside
the wild range of *narbonensis*.

Nowadays, this variety is classified as var.
minor and is still grown in countries like India,
Afghanistan and Pakistan. Sizes seem to have
remained the same in that category until
Roman times, when the modern broad bean
var. *major* (¼in long by⅜in wide) was born,
somewhere in the southwestern corner of Asia
on the Mediterranean fringe.

Primitive *faba* beans were black—Homer
(*c.*900 B.C.) mentions black-seeded beans in the
Iliad. Pale or buff-colored beans probably
originated in the Roman era, perhaps at the

same time as major varieties. In Roman elections, black beans were used to indicate no votes and white beans yes votes. Pale beans certainly existed in Europe in the sixteenth century—witness the lady shelling beans in Lucas van Valkenborch's *Allegory of Summer.*

The bean may be nutritious but it has acquired a reputation down the centuries of being a coarse, indigestible, fart-inducing, poor man's food, best reserved for animals, especially horses. Herodotus, the Greek historian from the fifth century B.C., called the broad bean *kuamos,* claiming that Egyptian priests regarded it as unclean, defiling even to handle.

It was certainly grown in Egypt from an early date and there was a strong association with death. Seeds have been recovered from Old Kingdom tombs of the third millennium B.C., and in classical Greece it had funereal, spectral associations. Funerals ended in beanfeasts and beans were used to exorcise houses haunted by the ghosts of the wicked.

One of the odder theories of Pythagoras, the mathematician and philosopher who lived a century before Herodotus, was that human souls turned into beans after death. The Roman *Pontifex Maximus,* or High Priest, was barred from eating or even mentioning beans because they were considered so inauspicious. That did not stop Roman politicians from distributing free beans before elections.

Bean ghost stories persisted well beyond Roman times. The Scots believed witches rode around on beanstalks and the Celts held *beanos* or beanfeasts to honor the fairies. If you saw a ghost, the best way to get rid of it was to spit at it with a bean.

But European consumers in the Middle Ages, in spite of its supernatural associations, continued to eat beans by the sackful, largely because they were the only edible beans available at a time when other nutritious vegetables were in fairly short supply. They could be dried, too, and eaten during winter without losing their nutritional value. The penalty for stealing beans or peas from an English field in the Middle Ages was death.

There is no evidence that beans were grown in China (now the world's leading producer, growing more than the rest of the world combined) before about A.D. 1200. They were probably introduced from western Asia along the silk trade routes and by 1500 were grown there on an extensive scale. Nineteenth-century travelers in China used numerous varieties of large-seeded, *major* varieties.

In the sixteenth century, large-seeded *faba* beans sailed to the New World, where they were unknown before Columbus and were planted by Spanish colonists and padres in Central and South America. Today, Brazil is a leading producer. In North America, where farmers were accustomed to native New World beans, they never really caught on; only recently have they been cultivated there on any notable scale.

Today, cultivated beans are divided into four main categories in descending order of size: var. *faba* or *major,* which we grow in our gardens; var. *equina,* the horse bean, grown for animal fodder; var. *minor,* the tic or pigeon bean and, very similar to *minor* but self-pollinating, var. *paucijuga,* extensively grown in Asia. *Faba* beans are subdivided into "Longpods," with up to eight seeds per pod, and "Windsors," with only about four.

PYTHAGORAS, GREEK PHILOSOPHER AND MATHEMATICIAN *c.*580–500 B.C.

ROMAN COPY OF GREEK BUST

Marble

Pinacoteca Capitolina

Palazzo Conservatori

Rome, Italy

When broad beans sailed to the Americas in the sixteenth century, they crossed with New World beans (*Phaseolus*) travelling the other way.

There are about fifty species in the *Phaseolus* genus, all native to the Americas and, of these, the three most important domestications are *Phaseolus vulgaris*, otherwise known as the common, french, navy, flageolet or snap bean, or haricot vert; *Phaseolus coccineus*, the scarlet runner bean; and *Phaseolus lunatus*, the Lima or butter bean.

Phaseolus beans have been part of the diet of Native American Indians for thousands of years, providing vital protein to complement the carbohydrate staples of potatoes and squashes, maize, and manioc, also known as cassava.

Vulgaris, the common french bean, grows wild down the spine of South America, from Mexico to Argentina, at heights between about 765 ½ and 2,624 ¾ yards. In Mexico it is a climbing plant that likes scrambling over forest trees and shrubs. It has narrow purple pods and small seeds about .2–.25in long.

Wild Andean varieties farther south have slightly bigger seeds. Seeds of cultivated plants dating back to 6,000 B.C., have been found in Peru and in deposits in the Tehuacan valley caves of Mexico's Puebla province from 4,000 B.C. But botanists are not able to agree exactly where in Central or South America the Pre-Columbian Indians first brought *vulgaris* into cultivation. It may well have been domesticated independently in a number of different places, at more or less similar dates, within its wild range. Indian cultivation spread it slowly into western North America—seeds that date to 300 B.C. have been found in New Mexico. With the arrival of more mobile Europeans in the sixteenth century, faster seed movement took place and crosses of Andean and Central American types expanded the germplasm.

The Lima bean, which has a long, wild range from Mexico to Argentina has a similar, diversified history. But the geographical range of the scarlet runner bean (*Phaseolus coccineus*) is much more restricted. It is a perennial, scrambling climber that grows in the cool, humid mountain regions of Mexico, Panama and Guatemala above about 1,968 ½ yards. Its flowers are scarlet and its seeds are very small, up to about ⅛in long; they taste like cultivated runners. The admittedly scanty archaeological evidence suggests it was domesticated much later than the common bean, perhaps in the third millennium B.C., and probably in Mexico.

The common bean, *vulgaris*, seems to have been the popular European choice in the early days. Only the climbing forms were planted, bush varieties did not appear until the eighteenth century, and scarlet runners were grown not to eat, but were used instead as ornamental exotics. Philip Miller, who ran the Chelsea Physic garden in the early 1700s, is credited with being the first Englishman to have advocated cooking and eating their green pods.

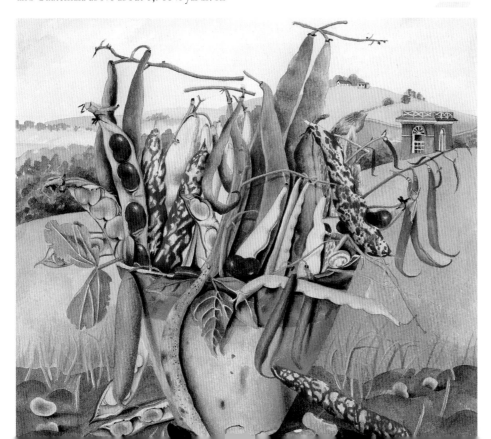

BEANS IN A FLOWER POT, 1995

E.B. WATTS

Acrylic on canvas

Private Collection

Cucumber, pumpkins, marrows, & squashes

Cucumis sativus *and* Cucurbita *genus of the* Marrow *family*

The "lodge in a garden of cucumbers" in Isaiah is the ubiquitous ramshackle shack of the Nile Valley or the Levant, from which an old watchman keeps a wary eye over his fruit and vegetables. In Biblical times it might have been made of reeds. Today, it is rusty, corrugated iron: a typical garden hut architecture for the acres of melons and cucumbers that grow around the southeast Mediterranean shore.

Cucumbers are natives of India. In Isaiah's day, the eighth century B.C., they were rare—perhaps even unknown—in the Levant. What Isaiah probably had in mind were small, green-fruited chate melons, *Cucumis chate*. They are bent and elongated, like cucumbers, but covered with soft, white hairs and have juicy, bitter flesh that can be eaten fresh, pickled or cooked. Like the sweet muskmelons, chates descend from the wild, annual, weedy melons with plum-sized fruits that originated in sub-Saharan Africa, moved north into Asia, and became part of the near east native flora at a very early date. When we see cucumbers in the wonderful Egyptian wall paintings of the Tomb of Nakht at Western Thebes from 1,400 B.C., we are, in fact, on all the available palaeobotanical evidence, looking at chate melons.

William Tyndale, the Gloucestershire man who translated the Bible into English from the Hebrew in the sixteenth century, fell into the same trap: he called *mikshah* a "garden of cucumbers" in Isaiah and in Numbers he had the Israelites longing for the cucumbers (*kishuim*) they had left behind in Egypt—it was really chate pickling melons that they missed.

So where was it that cucumbers originated, and when were they first domesticated? The best guess is that they arrived in the Mediterranean region rather late, sometime during the first millennium B.C., more or less in Greek Classical times.

They were probably first cultivated in India in the foothills of the eastern Himalayas where a wild form of cucumber, *Cucumis sativus* var. *hardwickii* still grows—but whether *hardwickii* is a true progenitor, or a wilding, or a bit of both, no one is quite sure. It is fully interfertile with cultivated cucumbers, and has small, spiny, nasty-tasting fruit full of cucurbitacins (the turpenoid compounds responsible for bitterness in cucumber leaves and fruit).

It is fairly difficult for archaeologists to tell seeds of cucumbers and melons apart. But melon seeds have been identified in Stone Age sites in India (*c.*4000 B.C.) and in China (*c.*3000 B.C.). Cucumber seeds are first reliably reported in western Asia very much later (at Nimrud in Assyria, 715–600 B.C.). They do not appear to have arrived in China until about 200 B.C. This fits in with a scenario in which wild cucumbers speciated away from wild melons in niches in the eastern Himalayas, were improved under cultivation in northern India, then spread east and west in the cultivated melon's wake.

By Greek and Roman times, cucumbers were being grown and eaten round the Mediterranean basin. Seeds were probably taken from the Levant to Egypt and Greece by Phoenician merchants sailing out of what is now the Lebanon; then Greek colonizers planted them in Sicily, Italy and North Africa.

The Roman empire extended their range farther, to northern Europe; even (research at Fishbourne Palace in West Sussex suggests) as far as Britain. Cucumbers are warm weather plants, and dislike temperatures below 50°F. They can be grown in the open in the British Isles after all risk of frost is past. In Italy, the Romans grew them like vines—climbing over a pergola and giving shade—and a favorite trick was to enclose the fruits in hollow canes, or in plaited wicker or grass sheaths, so that they grew in fantastic forms of men and animals, or snakes. The emperor Tiberius had a passion for cucumbers and liked to eat them, if he could, all the year round. His gardeners grew them in portable, cold frame baskets covered with lapis specularis (perhaps mica)

And the daughter of Zion is left as a cottage in a vineyard, as a lodge in a garden of cucumbers, as a beseiged city.

Isaiah, 1:8

and wheeled them in and out according to the weather. After the spring equinox (roughly March 21st) the baskets were left outside in permanent positions. Pliny the Elder, the Roman admiral overwhelmed in the Bay of Naples by the Vesuvian eruption in A.D. 79, wrote extensively of the culture of cucumbers; as did his contemporary Columella, who farmed at Cadiz in Spain. Neither made any mention of using artificial ground heat to force them on.

Were hotbeds for melons and cucumbers known to the Romans? They were probably an Arab invention. Ibn Bassal, gardener to the Sultan of Toledo in the eleventh century, left the first written description of how to make them: in December or January, against an east wall, with a five-foot-thick layer of fresh mule or horse dung (pigeon dung for extra combustion) and the seeded surface covered with cabbage or cauliflower leaves in order to retain the heat.

As Rome declined, so did the culture of cucumbers. At least until the Renaissance,

LA MARCHANDE DE FRUITS ET LÉGUMES, 1630
LOUISE MOILLON
1610–1696
Oil on canvas
Louvre
Paris, France

ROMAN MOSAIC OF CUCUMBERS FROM THUSDRUS (EL JEM IN TUNISIA)
Bardo Museum
Tunis, Tunisia

139

with padres and colonists along the Spanish Main and up and down the Pacific coast, from California to Chile.

In the nineteenth century, it was discovered that unpollinated female flowers could make sweeter, if smaller, cucumbers and that selected all female plants could be grown under glass during the winter, when pollinators were absent, and still produce tasty seedless fruit. Today, cucumbers are grown as a major crop, in the open and under glass, throughout the warm, moist regions of the world. They are not very nutritious, consisting mostly of water, but are always popular in sandwiches and salads.

Gherkins are cucumbers picked small, so they are Old World plants too. The spherical-fruited, West Indian gherkin, *Cucumis anguria*, now widely cultivated throughout the Caribbean, used to be thought a New World native. In fact it arrived in Brazil before about 1650 with slave traders from Angola and descends from a much spinier, even more bitter species, *Cucumis longipes*, which still grows wild in southwest Africa and with which it is fully interfertile.

Pumpkins, marrows and squashes, all members of the *Cucurbita* genus (and like melons and cucumbers, of the natural order *Cucurbitaceae*) are exclusively American in origin and were unknown in Europe before Columbus—although they were introduced to the Old World within fifty years of his first voyage. They come in a bewildering number of shapes and sizes, from the small zucchini or courgette (the immature fruit of the vegetable marrow) to world record-breaking giant pumpkins, *Cucurbita maxima*, weighing 1,000 pounds or more.

northern European consumers were as suspicious of them as of other non-native fruits, which they associated with autumn, dysentery, and the ague (malaria, a killer then, even in Britain). But cucumbers were grown and eaten in England in Henry VIII's day, and Columbus included them in the seed collection that he took with him to the New World. Planted in Haiti, they grew with astonishing speed; their culture soon spread

The American cucurbits are thought to have evolved at a very early date in Central and South America from gourd-like fruits with bitter flesh and edible seeds. It was these oil- and protein-rich seeds that early American Indians were after when they brought them into cultivation, or anyway tolerated them on their middens. Cultivars with better-tasting flesh were a later improvement.

Cucurbita pepo—the species from which cultivars of round, orange pumpkins, vegetable marrows, summer squashes and gourds derive—was one of the earliest Indian crops of the New World. Seeds have been found in 8,000-B.C. burial caves in Mexico. By the time of Columbus' arrival, Native Americans were growing *pepo* pumpkins along with maize and beans all the way up the east coast of North America as far as Canada. The Pilgrim Fathers who made landfall at Cape Cod, Massachusetts in 1620, had little experience in farming and gardening, least of all with native plants. Half their party died in the first winter and many more would have perished in the second if the Patuxet Squanto Indians had not shown them how to grow pumpkins among their corn, using herring as fertilizer. In October 1621 they held their first thanksgiving meal, with boiled pumpkins on the table (later, the settlers learned to cut off the fruit's top, scoop out its flesh and seeds, fill it with milk and roast it whole until the milk was absorbed). Pumpkin pie has been a part of the Thanksgiving Day celebration ever since.

The giant pumpkin, *Cucurbita maxima*, was a staple of the Peruvian Incas. Evidence for its cultivation comes from sites dating from 2,000 B.C. in coastal Peru, though there is no evidence that it grew north of the equator before Columbus. Today, in the U.S., they grow well in the colder northern latitudes.

The butternut or Winter Squash, *Cucurbita moschata,* prefers the humid, sub-tropical south, while the Green-Striped Cushaw or Ayote, *Cucurbita argyrosperma*, thrives in semi-desert conditions in Arizona. Evidence suggests both were cultivated in southern Mexico from around 5,000 B.C.

The Fig-leaved Gourd, *Cucurbita ficifolia*, grows in the Mexican and Andean uplands as far south as Chile and is the same plant eaten by Peruvian Indians in 3,000 B.C.. It came to Europe before 1613, when it was illustrated in *Hortus Eystettensis*, the garden book of the prince bishop of Eichstatt, Bavaria.

PECAN AND
PUMPKIN PIE

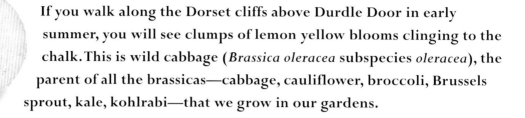

Cabbage

Brassica oleracea *of the* Cabbage *family.*

If you walk along the Dorset cliffs above Durdle Door in early summer, you will see clumps of lemon yellow blooms clinging to the chalk. This is wild cabbage (*Brassica oleracea* subspecies *oleracea*), the parent of all the brassicas—cabbage, cauliflower, broccoli, Brussels sprout, kale, kohlrabi—that we grow in our gardens.

Wild cabbage (sometimes called sea cabbage) looks like purple sprouting broccoli. It has wavy, red-tinged leaves, a sturdy, branching stem, and roots well anchored to the chalky cliffs—a climber was saved by grabbing this plant in the 1980s. It is fairly rare and often well out of reach, growing on only a handful of sites, all chalk or limestone sea cliffs from North Wales around the south coast to Kent. Across the Channel, it ranges from Guernsey down the Atlantic coasts of France and Spain. Other closely related species crop up along the Côte d'Azur: *B. robertiana* in Sardinia and Corsica; the white flowered *B. insularis* in North Africa; and in the eastern Mediterranean, *B. cretica,* which sometimes produces white flowers.

Is it a true native species that grew again when the Ice Age receded from Britain 15,000 years ago? Probably not. Recent studies of thirty different sites suggest the Romans or Saxons brought it over from the Continent. It mostly grows near towns or villages, or near invasion/garrison routes like Dover. It was an early garden escape.

Brassica oleracea is a polymorphic plant—one that can assume a variety of different forms. The six main groups of kitchen garden cultivars

include the non-heading kales (*acapitata*), heading cabbages (*capitata*), swollen-stemmed kohlrabi (*gongylodes*), Brussels sprouts (*gemmifera*), broccoli (*cymosa*), and cauliflower (*botrytis*). All have been carefully developed, or "ennobled," by centuries of seed or mutant selection by gardeners. Each group breeds true, but can quickly revert if inoculated with pollen from another group. Seed producers grow different brassicas in carefully segregated plots, otherwise chaos ensues.

In a fascinating experiment in the 1930s in Reading, W.F. Giles grew wild cabbages from seed collected from the English cliffs, and reported what happened in a wartime lecture to the Royal Horticultural Society:

"The plants were much finer than when found growing wild, because they had had garden cultivation. Most of the plants raised were quite green in foliage, although a few were slightly tinged red, and one or two of them showed some tendency to produce loose shoots or sprouts on the stem.

"In order to satisfy myself that these plants of the wild *B. oleracea* would cross with the cultivated forms, controlled crosses were made between these wild plants and the following: Brussels Sprouts, Cabbage, Curled

BRASSICA OLERACEA,
WILD CABBAGE

*Durdle Door
Dorset, U.K.*

Scotch Kale, Purple Curled Kale, Russian Kale, Savoy, Kohlrabi, and White Heading Broccoli. All the crosses proved fertile, and some very interesting hybrid plants were raised in the F1 generation.

"From these F1 plants specimens were selected, and these were seeded under protection and control, and allowed to self-fertilise. They all produced seed…although there was more or less evidence of some of the characteristics of the cultivated forms used in the crosses, practically all the plants were absolutely nondescript, the majority showing the characteristics of the Wild Kale very prominently."

In another Reading experiment, single plants of various garden cultivars, including heading cabbages and variegated kales, were planted in a square and allowed to cross-pollinate. Again, the work of centuries was wiped out in a generation; the heading characteristic disappeared, and the dominant, branching, wild cabbage gene took over.

The evolution of *Brassica* cultivars is a long, ongoing story. As late as the 1920s for example, broccoli, hitherto unknown in the United States, was introduced to New York by Italian immigrants. One elegant theory has linked the winter-hardy kales, cabbages and kohlrabis with the northern subspecies, and the more tender cauliflowers and some broccolis (*Romanesco* and *Calabrese*) with *Brassica cretica* from the Mediterranean.

The classical Greeks were familiar with cabbages and the Romans liked eating them, or at least believed they did you good. Cato "the Censor," that rugged upholder of the old Republican virtues against soft Hellenism in the 2nd century B.C., devoted a long passage to the

plant in his *De Re Rustica*, mostly on the lines that cabbage is good for you, and strongly recommended it cooked or pickled.

Pliny the Elder, in his *Historia Naturalis*, published two years before he died in the volcanic eruption that overwhelmed Pompeii and Herculaneum (as admiral of the Roman fleet stationed at Misenum, he put to sea to rescue friends caught on the shore of the Bay of Naples), described a swollen-stemmed plant very like kholrabi, and leaf cabbages, and headed cabbages 12in across. His list of cabbage-related medicines totals a daunting eighty-seven. By an odd coincidence, the

countryside round Naples and Vesuvius, where Pliny died, is now one of the main broccoli producing areas of the world.

The Germans grew red and white headed cabbages in the 1100s and crinkly leaved, mildly flavored Savoys in the 1500s; they also appear regularly in sixteenth-century Dutch and Italian art. The first mention of cabbage in English is in William Turner's *A New Herball,* in 1551. Turner saw it growing at Dover and he called it Sea Cole. At that time it seems to have been a wild food of the rural poor.

Broccoli, some say, arrived in Italy from the eastern Mediterranean in the seventeenth

JANUARY KING CABBAGE

ALISON COOPER
Watercolor on paper
Private Collection

STILL LIFE

1571–1610

MICHELANGELO
MERISI DA
CARAVAGGIO

Private collection

century. Its ancestor may (or may not) have been *B. cretica*. In his *Garden Dictionary* 1724, Phillip Miller, curator of the Apothecaries' Garden at Chelsea, called it "Italian asparagus."

Cauliflower was introduced by the Moors to Spanish gardens in the fifteenth century, and its first mention in English is by John Gerard in his *Herball* (1597). He called it *colieflore*, and recommended it be started on a hot dungheap

in early spring. This was one of the few gardening tips that the fraud, Gerard, got right. An unscrupulous barber and surgeon from London, he plagiarized and botched an unfinished English translation of Dodoens, laced it with myth and misinformation and produced a bestseller that, down the centuries, has been an hilarious source of error. Rembert Dodoens, a professional herbalist from the

Low Countries, had illustrated a crude cauliflower in his first herbal, entitled *Cruÿdeboeck*, published in 1554, and recorded: "The seeds came from Cyprus, because they would not ripen well elsewhere, being too sensitive to the cold."

Kohlrabi, a tough plant equally at home and flavor-retentive in hot semi-desert or high alpine valleys, probably developed from a thickly stemmed mutant of *B. oleracea*. A plant very like it was described by Pliny—he called it a "Corinthian turnip"—it reappeared in northern Europe in the fifteenth century. In England it was still a novelty in Victorian times and even today it remains a minority taste.

Brussels sprouts were first recorded in Belgium in about 1750. They probably descend via Cottager's Kale, a very old and hardy type, close to Wild Kale, with a tendency to form buttoning sprouts down its stem. Brussels sprouts, unless their seed is carefully selected, revert to forming loose sprouts (but these sprouts, if left to open and grow, can produce delicious edible shoots in the spring).

Wild cabbage can taste as good as garden cabbage if the leaves are picked young enough, in April. Because of their salty taste, it is worth scalding them before boiling. Later in the season, when the leaves turn purplish, they become bitter. Geoffrey Grigson records in his *Englishman's Flora* that wild cabbage used to be sold in the shops at Dover, but that the leaves needed repeated washings, and two boilings, before they were fit to eat.

The English have long been mocked for overcooking their brassicas—cabbage smells and English institutions go hand in hand—but some peasant dishes of France and Germany

require well-cooked cabbage too, not least cabbage soup (*soupe aux choux*), popular as far south as Provence since medieval times. This is a vegetable stew with cabbage leaves and pickled pork (or joints of salted goose or duck preserved in their own fat), covered with water and left to simmer for up to four hours. If begun at breakfast time, as Jane Grigson records in her *Vegetable Book*, the dish will be ready for lunch.

Sauerkraut, which is known as *choucroute* in France, takes even longer to cook. Finely shredded cabbage leaves are pickled in a stone crock or wooden cask, with sea salt and juniper berries, for up to three weeks, until the brew stops frothing. The Germans eat it with pork, smoked goose or sausages (especially frankfurters).

FOOD AND DRINK COOKING, C.1830

GEORGE CRUIKSHANK JUNIOR

The cabbage was once the staple of English cuisine and it was popular to cook the vegetable whole

Leaf beet & beetroot

Beta vulgaris *of the* Goosefoot *family*

You can find wild Sea Beet (*Beta vulgaris* subspecies *maritima*) growing just above the high tide mark on bare sand or shingle, even out of old sea walls, round the temperate coasts of Europe and western Asia from the Canaries to the Arabian Sea. It is a fairly nondescript perennial, reaching two feet high, with edible, dark green, leathery leaves and spiky clusters of green flowers that appear from June to September.

The growing parts are sometimes tinged with red. You probably would not give it a second glance, least of all want to eat it (although, according to Geoffrey Grigson, residents of the Isle of Wight used to call it sea spinach and cook it with pork or bacon). But it is the wild progenitor of all the many and various beets that have variated and been selected by man since prehistoric times: leaf beets for salads and spinach, root beets for cooking, fodder beets for animals, sugar beets for sweetening our food and drink. The thin, stringy roots of wild beets contain substances like saponin and betaine, which give them a harsh, bitter taste.

The earliest beets were cultivated for their leaves and have evolved down the centuries into succulent plants without swollen roots, eaten in their first season as annuals: what nowadays we call Spinach Beet, Perpetual Spinach, Seakale Beet or Swiss Chard. But exactly when and where these leaf beets were first domesticated is uncertain. Leaf and root vegetables, unlike charred cereal grains and fruit stones, do not oblige palaeobotanists by surviving for thousands of years in archaeological contexts; buried evidence for cultivated beets in pre-Classical times is, unfortunately, nonexistent.

The earliest literary reference for beet comes from eighth-century B.C. cuneiform tablets from Babylon, and it is likely that the first domestications of beet occurred, along with other vegetables like cabbages, carrots, chicory, globe artichokes, turnips, and asparagus, in the Fertile Crescent area between the Nile and the Indus, perhaps sometime during the second millennium B.C.. This was long after fruits like dates, pomegranates, olives and grapes were grown in early Mesopotamian gardens.

By Greek classical times, leaf beets seem to have become well-established in the Mediterranean basin, both for medicinal purposes and as potherbs for flavoring. They are mentioned by both Theophrastus and Aristotle, who wrote of a red chard variety (a color inherited from the sometimes red-tinged, wild plant). The Greek word for beet was *teutlion*. Cultivars with swollen red taproots—beetroots—are thought not to appear until Roman imperial times and the beginning of the

Christian era. Some botanists, however, suggest a much later date for their introduction—the late Middle Ages—on the grounds that no certain documentary evidence for their existence occurs before about the sixteenth century. But "Roman Beet" was the name for red beetroot in Tudor times, and many of the old Roman root vegetables like radishes, parsnips, turnips and carrots remained largely forgotten and unsown in northern Europe for 1,000 years from the fall of the Empire until the Renaissance. Cabbages and onions, which persisted as staples right through the Dark Ages, were what the medieval peasant fell back on for his survival if corn stocks fell low.

An unwelcome, wild plant characteristic of beets that needed to be bred out over the centuries is what botanists call "synaptospermy": fruits growing together on flower stalks to make a tight, composite seed ball. In very dry conditions in the wild (as in the Middle East) it is beneficial for plants to germinate and grow in close groups rather than in scattered positions;

SUGAR BEET, EAST ANGLIA, 1973

EDWARD BURRA

Watercolor on paper

Private Collection

but it is less helpful in the garden or farmer's field. Modern beets are "one seeded" types.

By the sixteenth and seventeeth centuries, European herbalists were describing many different types of root and leaf beets, red beetroots among them. John Gerard, in his 1597 *Herball*, recorded his delight with some seeds of "great red Beete or Romaine Beete" that a merchant friend called "Master Lete" had brought him from overseas. He planted them in 1596, and they grew 12ft high (or so claimed the not always reliable Gerard). The leaves were good to eat with oil, vinegar and pepper:

but what might be made of the beautifull roote (which is to be preferred before the leaves, as well in beautie as in goodnesse) I referre unto the curious and cunning cooke, who no doubt when he hath had the view thereof, and is assured that it is both good and holsome, will make thereof many and divers dishes both faire and goode.

BEETS (*BETA VULGARIS*), 1988
JESSICA TCHEREPNINE
Watercolor on paper
Private Collection

The yellow-rooted mangel (also called mangold and mangle-wurzle) originated in Germany. It occurred in the Rhineland in the 1750s, a chance hybrid between a red, swollen rooted garden beet and a white stemmed chard, and was first used for cattle feed in 1787. The fresh roots are in fact mildly toxic to stock and need to be lifted and kept in a clamp for a couple of months before feeding, but they have the advantage over swedes in that they do not taint milk. In the days before swathes of northern Europe were dedicated to grass or maize silage, farmers grew acres of old fashioned mangels, their roots sitting up high on the ground like beetroots, to feed their winter stock.

In 1747, Andreas Marggraf, German chemist and member of the Berlin Academy of Sciences, published an account of how to extract sugar (hitherto obtainable only from sugar cane grown in the tropics) from plants indigenous to Europe, especially beetroot and carrots. He demonstrated that their dried roots, cooled down after being boiled in alcohol, deposited crystals exactly similar to those of sugar cane (His experiments were memorable in another way too: he pioneered the employment in chemistry of the microscope, with which he picked out the tiny sugar crystals in the roots). One of Marggraf's students, Archard, trialed beets for sugar production near Berlin. He crossed pigmented garden root beets with chard to produce white-rooted plants, and by 1775, when the first sugar beets were introduced to France, he had managed to get the sugar content in one of his cultivars, which he called *Weisse Schlesiche Rube*, up to about six percent (modern varieties average over eighteen percent) sucrose.

The first sugar extracting factory was set up in Silesia, in 1802, at a time when the price of West Indian sugar was at an all-time high and English sugar millionaires, like the slave owner William Beckford, who built Fonthill Abbey in Wiltshire with a tower higher than Salisbury cathedral's, lived like nabobs. Beckford built a high wall (still visible in places) round his estate, not to fence deer in, but to keep foxhunters, whom he detested, out.

Napoleon gave every encouragement to the new crop and set up institutes for its culture in order to sabotage the English trade, or at any rate the continental blockade by Nelson's navy.

As the war drew to a close, West Indian sugar cane prices were on the floor, planters were going bust, and Beckford was forced to sell up at Fonthill. His jerry-built tower later collapsed; its implosion blew a valet out of a passage in the adjoining abbey like a cork out of a popgun.

Today, nearly half the world's sugar comes from sugar beet. The former USSR is by far the biggest producer, followed by Germany and North America, where the first sugar beet factory was set up in California in 1870.

DIGGING BEETROOT I, 1911

LEON WYCZOLKOWSKI
1852–1936
Oil on canvas
Muzeum Narodowe
Warsaw, Poland

Carrot

Daucus carota *of the* Carrot *family*

It comes as no surprise that the cultivated, biennial carrot descends from the wild, weedy, annual carrot whose various subspecies (13 have been identified to date) range across just about the whole temperate zone of the Old World.

It is not so easy, however, to determine when and where the carrot changed from annual weed to biennial vegetable and how it acquired its fleshy, colored, undivided taproots which, filled with vitamins A and C, sugar and carbohydrates, have made it one of the most cultivated root crops on the planet—far more widely grown than its popular umbellifer relatives: parsnips, parsley and celery.

Roots of wild carrots tend to be thin, stringy, well-forked for good anchorage and water uptake, more or less inedible, and white. In Britain, they grow in waste places, beside paths or railway lines, or on dunes and in summer limestone meadows beside the sea. Unlike cultivated carrots, they flower in their first year. You can see their parasol-like umbels outgrowing the grass to catch the sun: first pink-, then white-topped as the flowers develop, and flat or convex turning to concave as the seed-heads form. Hence their local name "birds' nests," noted by John Gerard in his 1597 *Herball*. The seeds have tiny spines that cling to the fur of dispersing animals, or to each other: if you want to sow them thinly, you need to separate them first by rubbing them in dry ashes or sand.

Wild and cultivated carrots can interbreed—carrot seed breeders go to great lengths to stop their crops becoming contaminated by feral carrots—but cultivated carrots, like turnips and kohlrabi, can not survive for long unaided in the wild. The savory, fleshy, water-and-sugar-storing taproots they put down in their first season (they flower and seed in their second) make them prime targets for winter-attack by animals, mostly rabbits, and frost. Stringy and unpalatable wild roots survive.

In the days before the laws of heredity were properly understood, it used to be thought that if you grew wild carrots in your garden for long enough, they would eventually turn into cultivated carrots. The French horticulturalist and founder of the famous nineteenth-century seed nursery in Paris, M. Vilmorin, reported in an 1840 paper to the Royal Horticultural Society in London that in six years from 1833, starting with wild seed from white-rooted plants, he had managed to grow thicker, biennial, red-rooted carrots, but that they nevertheless remained coarse, fibrous, forked and not very tasty. His partial success had nothing to do with cultivation, everything to do with the wild carrot's gene pool that enabled him to fix the genomes he selected. Vilmorin's carrots had varied. He simply selected seed from biennial, red-rooted variations.

Daucus carota

Where did wild carrots originate, and where were they first brought into cultivation? Nikolai Vavilov, the Soviet plant geneticist whose teams of researchers scoured the planet in the 1930s for new plants to feed the Russian Revolution, found an abundance of wild carrots in Afghanistan and Turkestan, and concluded that the Hindu Kush region of central Asia was their original home. Carrots with red or purple roots still grow wild there.

These may have been the first to have been improved by selective cultivation, giving rise to so-called "eastern" or Asiatic carrots with down-covered, gray-green leaves and reddish-purple (sometimes yellow), forked roots containing the pigment anthocyanin, which turns red, violet or blue depending on the acidity of the cell sap. "Western" or carotene-pigmented carrots, with less downy, greener leaves and orange, yellow, or white single

STILL LIFE

JUAN SANCHEZ
COTAN
1560–1627
Private Collection

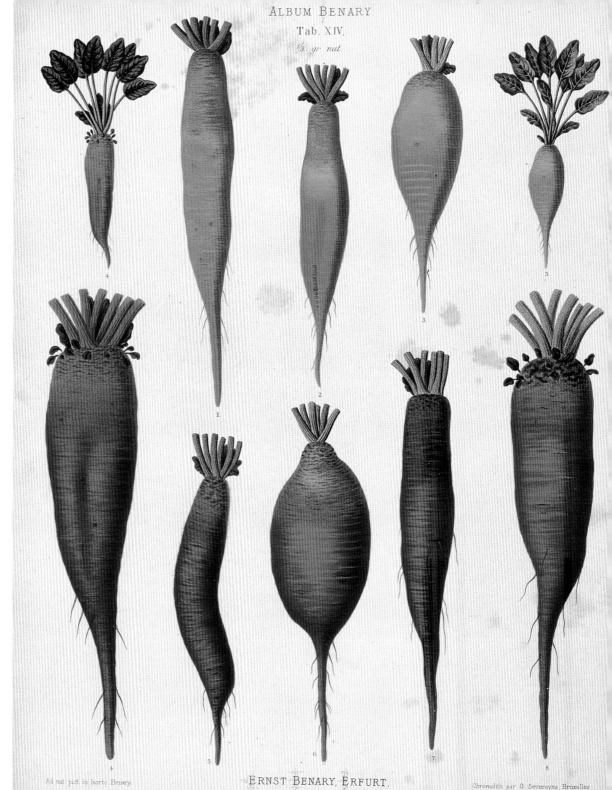

Ad nat. pict. in horto Benary.

ERNST BENARY, ERFURT.

Chromolith par G. Severeyns, Bruxelles.

taproots, developed later. According to Vavilov they came from "eastern" carrots, from the general area of Turkey and Asia Minor and perhaps from mutants that had dropped the anthocyanin. The orange carotene of "western" carrots, broken down by the mucous membranes of our stomachs, is a source of the Vitamin A we require for healthy optic nerves.

When were carrots domesticated? The archaeological evidence is frustratingly scanty. Vegetable and root crops, unlike cereal grains and fruit stones, are highly perishable and stand little chance of charring and being preserved. Carrot seeds have turned up in Neolithic (3,000 to 2,000 B.C.) settlements in Switzerland and southern Germany, but it looks as though it was only the seeds (possibly the umbels and leaves too) that were gathered by early man for eating; the roots were left in the ground. The best guess is that carrots, along with other vegetables like beet, cabbage, chicory, endive, turnip, globe artichoke and asparagus, were in a second wave of vegetables taken into cultivation in the Fertile Crescent (Nile to the Indus) around the beginning of the first millennium B.C. Melons, watermelons, leeks, garlic, onions and lettuces had preceded them into Babylonian or Egyptian vegetable gardens by perhaps 1,000 years.

There is no good evidence that the Greeks grew taprooted carrots, colored or white. They had words for plants with edible roots— *sisaron*, *staphulinos* and *elaphoboscon*—but they were probably parsnips or cluster-rooted skirrets. Skirrets are natives of damp ground from central Europe to Siberia and south to Iran, and their sweet, floury roots have been cultivated since ancient times. There is no doubt that Pliny, in his first-century A.D.

description of *pastinaca* (which he said was the same as the Greek *staphulinos*) was thinking of parsnips. One assumes that the Romans, at least after the Midthridatic wars in the 60s B.C., must have come across cultivated carrots in the southeastern corner of their empire. But it is not until the second-century A.D. that the Latin word *carota* first occurs—in the writings of Galen, the Levantine-Greek medical author who came to Rome in early A.D. 160 and in a cookbook from A.D. 230, Caelius Apicius's *De Re Coquinaria*. Galen had two names for the carrot—*daucus* and *carota*—and clearly distinguished it from the parsnip, *pastinaca*. In his eighteenth-century classification of plants, Linnaeus used both names: *daucus* as the generic and *carota* as the specific.

We know from written documents that purple (called "red" in the sources before 1700) and yellow carrots were being cultivated in Iran and Northern Arabia in the tenth century, and in Syria in the eleventh century. Yellow carrots grew largely above ground. The range of colored carrots expanded with Islam along the coast of North Africa and up into Spain (twelfth century), thence to Sicily and the Languedoc. They were in Italy in the thirteenth century, Germany and the Netherlands in the fourteenth, and in England in the fifteenth century. Contemporary artists painted them as purple, or yellow-rooted. A good Flemish, sixteenth-century example is Lucas van Valkenborch's *Allegory of Summer*, which shows both colors. As time passed, yellow varieties prevailed over purple in popularity. The orange taproots that we all grow today made their first appearance in European art about the middle of the sixteenth century. It is thought they were first developed in the Low Countries, probably

CARROTS AND TURNIPS: FROM THE ALBUM BENARY
G SEVEREYNS
Chromolitho
Private Collection

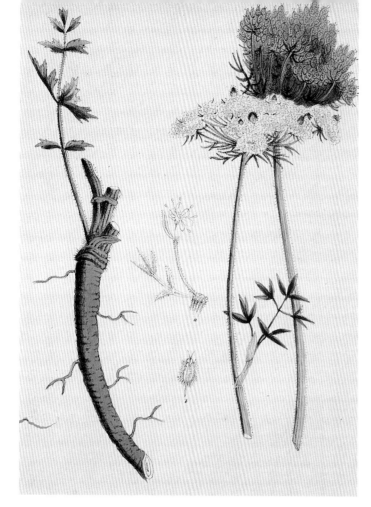

subspecies—in particular *D. carota* ssp. *maximus*, which has a Mediterranean range—chipped in its penny's worth of genes.

Whatever its origins, the Long Orange Dutch cultivar, first described in writing in 1721, is the progenitor of the orange Horn carrot varieties: Early Scarlet Horn (small, and still a good carrot for forcing), Early Half Long, and Late Half Long (big). All our modern, western, carotene carrots ultimately descend from these four cultivars.

Carrots were popular in England in Elizabeth I's time (when the range of vegetables to choose from was limited) and Shakespeare gave them an appreciative mention in his *The Merry Wives of Windsor*.

Calvinists on the run from Catholic persecution on the European continent grew them on the sandy soils round Sandwich in Kent, and in James I's day it was the fashion for ladies to trim their hats with carrot leaves.

Carrots were unknown in the New World, but in 1609, six years after James inherited the English throne as great-great-grandson of Henry VII, they were sown by his colonists in Virginia, whence they quickly escaped into the wild. Today, judging by the weedy colonies of feral carrots that have spread all over the continent, you would think they had been there for ever.

The first reports of carrots in China date from the thirteenth century, and in Japan from the eighteenth century. They were purple or yellow-rooted types, just like in Europe.

Today, carrots are grown all round the world, mainly in temperate zones, but also in the tropics and subtropics as a winter crop. China and the U.S. are the top producers in the world; Poland, Britain and France lead the way in Europe.

selected from yellow-rooted carrots. Oddly, white roots began to appear in pictures at about that time too, perhaps implying that there had been little attempt by western Europeans to domesticate the wild, white-rooted carrot until colored Moorish cultivars came along. But white roots never became very popular and, like the orange kind, they probably originated from yellow cultivars anyway, rather than directly from wild European species.

An alternative theory is that orange-rooted carrots were selected and fixed from yellow carrots in Holland, but that a wild carrot

**TURNIPS AND
CARROTS HO, PLATE
13,** FROM *CRIES OF
LONDON* (detail)
FRANCIS WHEATLEY
1747–1801
*Guildhall Library
Corporation of London,
U.K.*

Daucus carota

Parsnip

Pastinaca sativa *of the* Carrot *family*

The wild parsnip is the ancestor of all our garden cultivars. A plant that probably originated on the eastern Mediterranean rim, it now ranges throughout the whole of Europe as far north as Scandinavia. Since the voyages of discovery, it has colonized the New World and countries of the southern hemisphere, like Australia and New Zealand.

RECIPE FOR
SOUFFLÉED POTATOES
& PARSNIPS

Take ½ lb each of peeled and chopped potatoes and parsnips and boil until soft.

Mash with milk to a soft consistency, mix in two egg yolks, then salt, pepper and nutmeg to taste. Whisk the egg whites, fold in and put in a hot oven for 20 minutes.

SERVES FOUR.

Fairly common in the wild, the parsnip is an erect, branching biennial with hollow, shining, furrowed stems, yellow-green leaves and stately, high-summer umbels of yellow blooms up to 47in above the ground. You can find it in Britain beside roads, tracks and railway lines and in weedy disturbed ground like quarries, field margins and fallow set aside. It especially enjoys chalky grassland. The roots are tough, wiry, dry, short and fairly inedible; the seeds pleasantly aromatic.

The first wild parsnips were probably brought into cultivation, at a date and by persons unknown, as flavoring or medicinal herbs. The wild roots are sweet and parsnip-smelling, and the crushed leaves and stems give off the distinctive parsnip aroma. They could have been used as potherbs (although some modern cooks advise against parsnips in stews, especially vegetable stews: their flavor can be too overpowering). A decoction of the wild roots is said to help bowel movement and urinal discharge, and an oil extracted from the seeds to soothe intermittent fevers, such as malaria.

Parsnips eaten as vegetables with fleshy, swollen tap roots and high sugar and starch content evolved much later. But when? One theory is that these swollen-rooted parsnips did not appear until the later Middle Ages; another that the Greeks and Romans knew it and grew it, as a root vegetable. The difficulty, in the pre-Linnaean era, is knowing what the names meant. The Greeks grew plants with edible roots that they called *sisaron*, *staphulinos* and *elaphoboscon*. These may have been parsnips or cluster-rooted skirrets. Skirrets are natives of damp ground from central Europe to Siberia and south to Iran and have been cultivated for their sweet, floury roots since ancient times.

There seems little doubt that Pliny the Elder, in his first-century A.D. description of *pastinaca* in his *Naturalis Historia*, meant parsnips, not carrots. He said that the Greeks called them *staphulinos*, that they could be grown from seed or transplants, had a peculiar, indestructible flavor and that the Emperor Tiberius, who had a passion for exotic vegetables, put them on the Roman food map by importing plants every year from the banks of the Rhine in Germany.

De Re Coquinaria, the recipe book

posthumously compiled in the name of Caelius Apicius, a Roman celebrity cook living in the first-century A.D., implies that the Romans cultivated parsnips, and enjoyed eating them. A Roman still life fresco shows what appears to be a swollen-rooted fresh parsnip on a plate with olives, beside a glass cup with five eggs and a pomegranate hanging from a nail.

The parsnip's linguistic pedigree seems fairly straightforward. The Latin *pastinaca* (it is the same in modern Italian) became the Old French *pastenaie* or *pasnaie* (modern French *pasnais*) which was corrupted into the Old English *pasnepe* (from *pasnaie* and *neep*, a turnip). The German word is *pastinake*, and the Russian, *pasternak*, like the novelist.

Whether or not the swollen-rooted parsnip was invented by the Greeks and Romans, it certainly had a place in the later medieval gardens of northern Europe, although the roots were probably not as fleshy and swollen as in modern cultivars. The plant was useful in a number of ways. You could leave it in the ground all winter without damage—its starch becomes converted into sugar when the roots are frosted—and eat it in March and April, especially on Ash Wednesday during Lent, when it was cooked to accompany salt cod. Its sugary roots were fermented into wine, and were used to sweeten cakes, jams and a type of flour in the days when the only major sugar-source was honey. In England it was traditionally eaten with roast beef in the sixteenth and seventeenth centuries, when the South American potato was still regarded by the Protestant proletariat of northern Europe as something fit only for pigs and papists.

Charlemagne had listed the parsnip among the plants he required to be grown on his imperial estates in Europe in the ninth century, and the Fromond list (*c*.1525) of *Herbys necessary for a gardyn*—a shopping list for an English grandee's vegetable garden—included it in the root section, along with carrots, radishes, turnips and onions; all plants becoming increasingly popular during and after

STILL LIFE WITH
PARSNIP,
POMEGRANATE,
EGGS AND OLIVES
ROMAN FRESCO
The Romans cultivated parsnips, and enjoyed eating them

the Renaissance and providing some relief from the standard medieval fare of coleworts (kale) and leeks. Thomas Hill in his *Gardener's Labyrinth*, published in 1577, recommended sowing what he called "parsnep" seeds thinly in well-manured ground in high summer, for eating in Lent and again in February, and thinning them out, keeping them free from weeds, to achieve "some bignesse, at the least so big as the finger," which, by modern standards, is not very big. Hill had a high opinion of its medicinal properties, claiming that it:

removeth the venereal act, procureth Urine, and asswageth the Cholerick, sendeth down the Termes in Women; it profiteth the Melanchollicke, encreaseth good blood, helpeth the straightnesse of making water, amendeth stitches of the sides or plurisies, the bite of venemous beast, it amendeth the eating of Ulcers, the wearing of this root is profitable.

In southern Europe, parsnips are hardly grown or eaten at all—which is a real pity. They are very nutritious vegetables—as well as starch and sugar, they provide potassium and calcium and other mineral salts and trace elements. They are also well stocked in vitamins C and E.

At the end of the sixteenth century John Gerard, not normally noted for his accuracy, was quite right when he wrote:

The Parseneps nourish more than do the Turneps or the Carrots, and the nourishment is somewhat thicker, but not faultie nor bad....

Introduced to the West Indies in 1564, and thence to the Spanish Main, they only thrived at higher, colder altitudes where they frosted. They arrived in Virginia, in 1609, and were held in high esteem by American Indian tribes. But North Americans have never really taken European parsnips to their hearts, and they are only grown there on a small scale.

Gamote, a plant of a different genus, *Cymopterus montanus,* is sometimes called "wild parsnip" in the U.S. The Indians of the southwest and Mexico make a meal of its baked, ground roots.

With the rise of the potato, the growth of the West Indian sugar trade and a home-grown European sugar beet industry, the popularity of parsnips faded. Now they are produced on a large scale only in northern parts of Europe, particularly Germany.

Gardeners complain that parsnips are tricky to grow and modern breeding research has developed cultivars resistant to parsnip canker, a disease that rots the shoulders and crowns of growing plants, and to post-harvest browning, which is considered more of a problem with parsnips grown on sandy, rather than loamy, soils.

Pastinaca sativa

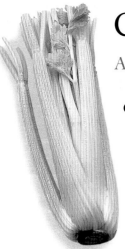

Celery, celeriac & parsley

Apium graveolens *and* Petroselinum crispum *of the* Carrot *family*

Our garden celeries and celeriacs descend from wild celery, an ancient plant. You can find it growing in moist, grassy places near the sea; brackish marshes and tidal flats are good places to look. It is fairly common, ranging from Denmark to North Africa and from Spain and Britain to the Himalayas.

A tallish (up to 24in) biennial plant, with hollow, grooved stems and shiny, yellow-green leaves, in its second season it carries numerous umbels that grow out of the leaf-axils and bear greeny-white flowers in high summer. All parts of the plant, especially the leaves, give off a pungent, distinctive celery smell. Eaten raw, the leaves and stems are bitter, and mildly poisonous.

Early gardeners between the Nile and the Indus, where horticulture began some 10,000 years ago, were attracted by its smell and flavor, and gathered and grew it, like parsley, as a flavoring potherb. Its seeds were used as a condiment, like salt and pepper. But at exactly what date it changed from a wild, gathered herb to a cultivated plant is hard to say. Probably rather late, perhaps sometime towards the end of the second millennium B.C., along with other "second wave" vegetables like cabbages, turnips, beet, asparagus and globe artichokes (leeks, onions, garlic and lettuce were all in the first wave, many hundreds of years before).

Preserved garlands of celery have been found on Egyptian mummies dating from the end of the New Kingdom (about 1,000 B.C.)—there is a fine example in the Agricultural Museum in Cairo, preserved like pressed flowers in the bone-dry atmosphere of the tombs—and the plant is often mentioned in Egyptian texts in medical contexts: boiled up with oil and sweet beer and swallowed four days in a row as a contraceptive; mixed with frankincense to heal bloodshot eyes; mixed with oil as a salve for sore joints. In Egypt, as later in Greece and Rome, it had funerary connections, perhaps because of its powerful, purifying smell.

Plants in classical texts—long before the days of Linnaeus and his binomial system of

PLINY THE ELDER

L'ILLUSTRATION

1855

Roman scientist and scholar dies while observing an eruption of Vesuvius, A.D. 79

Apium graveolens and *Petroselinum crispum*

naming plants—are not always easy to identify, and celery is no exception. When Homer (*c*.900 B.C.) wrote of "selino"' in the *Odyssey*, did he mean celery or its umbelliferous relation, parsley? Probably the former. The Greeks grew it in their gardens, ate its roots, made chaplets of the leaves for victors, and hung it in the rooms of the very ill or in the tombs of the dead. The Roman word was *apium*. Pliny the Elder, who was still revising his thirty-seven-volume *Naturalis Historia* when he was overwhelmed in the Bay of Naples by the 79 A.D. Vesuvian eruption, distinguished between wild and cultivated celery. At about the same date, Apicius, Roman gourmand and compiler of one of the world's first surviving cookbooks, was recommending *modicum apii viridis* ("a little green celery") as a garnish for a

STILL LIFE WITH DEAD BIRDS, FRUIT, AND VEGETABLES, 1602

JUAN SANCHEZ COTAN

1560–1627

Oil on canvas

Prado, Madrid, Spain

sauce, or a sprinkling of ground celery seed over fish before serving. Tastes have not changed: modern cooks use celery-seed mixed with salt—celery salt—as a condiment.

The development of celery as a vegetable with thick, sweet, succulent, blanched stalks is generally reckoned to have occurred in Italy at about the time of the Renaissance. In 1614, Giacomo Castelvetro, living in London on the run from the Inquisition in Italy and fairly disenchanted by the English diet, wrote nostalgically of the fruits, herbs and vegetables

of his native Italy, and how they were prepared and cooked. His *Brieve Racconto*, dedicated to Lucy Russell, Countess of Bedford, whom he hoped to enlist as a patron, is lively, simple, modern and accurate, and a much better read than John Gerard's more famous *Herball*, published seventeen years before.

Celery, wrote Castelvetro, should be sown in early spring in sifted ashes, then planted out about 7in apart in rich soil, and kept well-watered through the summer. In early autumn the plants should be lifted and put in a clamp

Apium graveolens and *Petroselinum crispum*

with the leaves sticking up "about four fingers above the ground," after about twenty days they will be blanched and good to eat. It should be served fresh, washed well, and with salt and pepper after meals.

In the Middle Ages in England, wild celery, known as "smallage" (from *ache*, old French for celery), was gathered as a medicinal herb. It was used as a laxative and diuretic, and to break up gall stones and relieve swellings. John Ray was an Essex blacksmith's son who wrote a three-volume *Historia Plantarum* and more or less founded modern botany with his distinction between monocotyledons and dicotyledons in flowering plants. He claimed that cultivated celery arrived in England from Italy via France during his lifetime (he died in 1705). He wrote: "Smallage transferred to culture becomes milder and less ungrateful, whence in Italy and France the leaves and stalks are esteemed as delicacies, eaten with oil and pepper"You can still buy smallage—wild celery with green, bitter, unblanched shoots known as *céleri à couper*—in French street markets, if you want to add a punchy flavor to soups and stews.

European colonists planted celery in their New World garden plots. Like carrots, it quickly escaped into the wild; judging by its feral range throughout North America today, you would think it had always been part of the native flora. In 1806, four varieties were offered in an American seed catalog. Today, stalk celery is grown all over the U.S., and in Canada too: states like New York, Michigan, California and Florida are premier producers.

In the old days, "blanching"—preventing chlorophyll from greening the stems (*petioles*) of celery and making them bitter—was

achieved by laborious earthing-up. Now, self-blanching varieties are widely available, as are cultivars with red, yellow or even pink stems.

Celeriac (*Apium graveolens* var. *rapaceum*) is sometimes called turnip-rooted celery. But this is a misnomer, for it is the lower stems, not the roots, that become bulbous and swollen. Its taste is mild and sweet and it seems to have originated as a garden variant of ordinary stem celery (confusingly known as var. *dulce*) on the Moslem, eastern Mediterranean rim. In 1575, the botanical writer, Rauwolf, recorded its

"CELERY" FROM
TACUINUM SANITATIS
EARLY FIFTEENTH
CENTURY
*Bibliothèque Nationale
Paris, France*

popularity amongst the Arabs.

There is no record of celeriac in Britain until the 1720s, when seeds were imported from Alexandria in Egypt and offered in a grower's catalogue. Elsewhere in central and eastern Europe it is widely cultivated, but in spite of being easy to grow it has remained largely a curiosity vegetable in Britain and North America.

Parsley (*Petroselinum crispum*), the world's most widely used potherb, probably originated on the eastern Mediterranean rim, where you can still find plants growing among the dry, barren rocks—though whether they are true natives, or long-escaped wildings, is unknown. It appears in Egyptian texts as "mountain parsley," not in cooking contexts, but as a cure for stomachache and, in one instance, mixed with celery, juniper berries and porridge "to contract the urine." Its actual effect, if anything, is diuretic: precisely the opposite.

The Greeks knew it and grew it and, when they remembered to, distinguished it from celery by calling it *oreoselinon* (mountain parsley) or *petroselinon* (rock parsley), which has evolved, via the medieval *petrocilium*, *petersylinge*, and *persele* into the French *persil* and our own parsley. Plato's pupil, Theophrastus (*c.* 300 B.C.) described the two cultivars that we grow today: the compact, curly leaved type that is now most popular in Britain, and the taller, flat-leaved, more flavorsome parsley favored by Mediterranean gardeners. But it probably did not feature as a potherb in Greek kitchens any more than in ancient Egyptian ones. It was grown, like celery, as a funerary plant: chaplets for mourners, wreaths for the dead, decorations for tombs and the like. The Greeks connected it with Persephone, goddess of the underworld, and Charon, ferryman of dead souls over the river Styx. They believed it sprang from the blood of a Greek hero, Archemorus, whose name translates as "harbinger of doom."

These grim associations persisted well beyond classical times: medieval peasants in northern Europe believed slow-to-germinate parsley seeds spent time off visiting the devil before coming up, and transplanting growing parsley plants (which were best sown on Good Friday) was strictly taboo.

The Roman attitude to parsley was more cheerful. They picked it green and interwove it onto flexible hoops of mulberry—or fig wood—to make garlands for birthdays, banquets and holidays. It was pliant, smelled sweet, and lasted for up to a month before turning the color of dried grass. Horace had seduction, not death, in mind when he wrote: "In my garden, Phyllis, is parsley for weaving gardlands, and a good store of ivy to bind back your hair and set off your beauty." According to Pliny the Elder, the Romans used both the leaves and seeds for seasoning food; he recommended scattering parsley leaves on the surface of villa stew ponds to cure sick fish.

Given the Roman zeal for plant hunting and transferral throughout their empire, it is quite possible that the Romans brought parsley to Britain. Charlemagne grew it on his imperial estates in the eighth century and in the fourteenth century the royal palace of Rotherhithe on the Thames put in a very large order for fourteen pounds of parsley seed—enough for an acre of ground—"or sowing in the King's garden in February" alongside leeks, onions and coleworts (cabbages). Henry VIII was particularly fond of white sauce with a parsley garnish.

Gathering wild parsley in Britain, though, can be as dangerous as picking mushrooms. Growing in damp, marshy places, it can easily be confused with the hemlock water dropwort, *Oenanthe crocata*, which can kill.

Hamburg parsley is grown for its edible root. Turnip or carrot-shaped, it has a rather subtle parsley/celeriac taste and originated in Germany in thesixteenth century. Phillip Miller, in charge of the Apothecaries' Garden at Chelsea, wrote in his *Gardeners' Dictionary* (1771) that Hamburg parsley "is now pretty commonly sold in the London markets, the roots being six times as large as the common Parsley. This sort was many years cultivated in Holland before the English gardeners could be prevailed upon to sow it. I brought the seeds of it from thence in 1727; but they refused to accept it, so that I cultivated it several years before it was known in the markets.'"

Globe & Jerusalem artichoke

Cyanara cardunculus *and*

Helianthus tuberosus *of the* Daisy *family*

The globe artichoke originated in the southern Mediterranean area and Near East. It is a cultivated version of the wild cardoon, *Cyanara cardunculus,* a tall, branching perennial thistle with prickly flower-heads and purple flowers, that grows wild from Crete to Spain and along the coast of North Africa. Another wild thistle, *Cyanara syriaca*, that grows along the eastern Mediterranean littoral, may well have added its penny's worth of genes to the artichoke's ancestry.

Grown in gardens, cardoons are enormous plants, reaching a height of 10ft with large, gray-green leaves. Their purple flowers are small in relation to their size. The edible parts, the young, fleshy leaf-stems that grow from a ground-level rosette, can be tied with brown paper and blanched like celery and are eaten raw or cooked.

As far back as the second millennium B.C., not only the stems, but also the immature flower heads of the cardoon made good eating and wild plants were brought into cultivation. By about 500 B.C., varieties with larger flower heads and shorter stalks had been selected and grown: the globe artichoke, a familiar vegetable in the classical world, was born.

The Greeks called it *kardos* or *skolumos* and the Romans *carduus*, which translates as a kind of thistle in both languages. It features in their literature and in Roman mosaics and wall paintings. For the Romans it seems to have had erotic connections—witness the painting of Priapus in the House of the Vettii at Pompeii.

The best artichokes were imported from Cordoba in Spain, or from Great Carthage in North Africa, where according to Dioscorides the plant was cultivated on a fairly large scale. His *Codex Vindobonensis*, a herbal written in the first century A.D. and copied for a Byzantine princess around 512 (sadly, only the princess' copy survives) describes and illustrates many

plants growing during the Roman period and is a marvelous source for exploring the flora of the ancient world—even if the drawings are only sixth-century copies.

Globe artichokes dislike frost and in Britain the dormant plants need to be straw-covered in winter. They were grown along frost-free Atlantic coasts of northern Europe (especially in Britanny) at least from the beginning of the sixteenth century, and before that in monastery gardens as culinary and ornamental plants.

During the Renaissance, still larger, more succulent flower heads may have been developed. They retained a reputation, inherited from Roman times, as an upper-class aphrodisiac and laxative; Henry VIII of England, it seems, couldn't get enough of them!

In his *Cruydeboek* or *History of Plants*, published in Antwerp in 1554, Rembert Dodoens, the painstaking botanist and Belgian physician at the Viennese court of Maximilian II, drew a distinction between what he called the "articoca" of Italy and the "cardoon," noting that the former was less spiny and a better food plant. John Gerard, who plagiarised Dodoens, illustrated a globe artichoke in his 1597 *Herball* and began a trend that was followed by numerous other seventeenth-century herbal writers. The same woodcuts were often used by successive authors, particularly the woodcuts of the house of Plantin in Antwerp, who published *Dodoens*.

MADONNA AND CHILD

GIOVANNI DELLA ROBBIA

1469–1529

Bas relief panel with artichoke detail

Tin-glazed earthenware

Bargello, Florence, Italy

John Parkinson, an English apothecary-botanist, quotes from the Greek writer of the fourth century B.C., Theophrastus, in his *Theatrum Botanicum* of 1640. He wrote that "the head of Scolymus is most pleasant, being boyled or eaten raw, but chiefly when it is in flower, as also the inner substance of the heads is eaten."

At the same time, at the court of Louis XIV in France, Francois Pierre de la Varenne was engaged in a cooking revolution, moving away from the heavy meat and almond stews that had dominated for so long. He believed that vegetables should exist on a plate in their own right, not just as ingredients for soups and stews. Popularising truffles and stuffed mushrooms, he was a particular fan of boiled globe artichokes with a lemony, buttery sauce—just as we eat them today.

Joseph de Tournefort was a Frenchman who practised medicine in London. In his *Institutiones Rei Herbariae* he made a determined, pre-Linnaean attempt at plant classification. He wrote in 1730: "The artichoke is well known at table….The French and Germans boil the heads as we do, but the Italians generally eat them raw with salt, oil and pepper."

The word "artichoke" seems to derive, via the old Italian word *articiocco* (Italians call artichokes *carciofi* today, and stuffed artichokes *carciofi alla Romana*), from the Arabic

Cyanara cardunculus and *Helianthus tuberosus*

al-kharshuf. In the seventeenth century, Giacomo Castelvetro spent the last five years of his life in England on the run from the Venetian Inquisition, and wrote nostalgically of the wonderful baby artichokes he remembered eating in the Po valley, raw or cooked. The raw ones, he said, needed to be about the size of walnuts—apple-sized was too big—and you could season them with salt, pepper and mature cheese. If they were bigger, the best thing to do was to cut off the top part of the leaves, grill the hearts over charcoal, and serve with salt, pepper, oil or melted butter, and a squeeze of bitter orange juice. Just writing about them, he said, made his mouth water.

Today, globe artichokes are grown all over the world. If you take the coast road south from Naples, perhaps to visit the temples at Paestum, you will see huge flat fields devoted to the crop, and irrigating gantries trundling up and down. The crop is over by May, and the tractors are out mowing the plants down to ground level.

The Jerusalem Artichoke, also called "topinambour" or "sunchoke," has nothing whatever to do with thistles, globe artichokes or cardoons, except that it is a member of the same *Compositae* family. It is a perennial sunflower that probably originated on the Great Plains of North America.

The early European settlers found it growing wild from the Canadian lakes to

THE PROMENADE OF A PHILOSOPHER, 1914

GIORGIO DE CHIRICO

1888–1978

Oil on canvas

Private Collection

Georgia in the south and from the Atlantic coast as far west as Saskatchewan.

It is not at all fussy about where it grows, but likes moist, sandy soils the best. The edible tubers can overwinter in frozen ground, under snow. In spring it grows stiff, tall stems, that in late summer (in North America anyway) are tipped with many small, yellow sunflowers above the last row of leaves. In England and other areas where the growing season is short, it often does not flower or even set seed.

Native Americans gathered and ate the artichoke's tubers, and perhaps farmed them too, long before the coming of colonial man. A 1588 account of the abortive Virginia settlement, planned and financed by Sir Walter Raleigh, lists "commodities there found and to be raysed" and refers to a root that the Algonquin Indians called *Kaishcucpenauk*— probably *tuberosus*.

In 1605, Native Americans were spotted cultivating it in Massachusetts by a Frenchman, Samuel de Champlain. Champlain explored the St Lawrence river, became the first governor of French Canada and first suggested the idea of a Panama canal, "by which the voyage to the South Sea would be shortened by 1,500 leagues." That summer he was surveying the Atlantic coast as far south as Cape Cod, looking for a site for the settlement that would later become Quebec. Champlain was an intriguing man, with twin ambitions that recall Columbus. It was written of him:

Two great objects eclipsed all others — to find a route to the Indies, and to bring all heathen tribes into the embraces of the Church, since, while he cared little for their bodies, his solicitude for their souls knew no bounds.

After his death his wife became a nun.

Champlain, in his account of the plant, said that the roots tasted like artichokes, and thus gave it half its name.

For centuries it was assumed that the other half of the artichoke's name, Jersualem, was a corruption of *girasole*, Italian for sunflower; but the name "Jerusalem artichoke" has in fact been shown to predate the first use of *girasole*, and the source is more likely to be Terneusen, a village on the Dutch coast between Antwerp and Ostend, whence artichokes were first brought to England in 1617.

Its other name, "topinambour," is even more adventitious. In 1613 six natives of the Brazilian Topinambous tribe were brought to France and paraded at the court of Louis XIII amid intense public interest. Enterprising barrow-boys in Paris, not knowing quite what to call the new vegetables, cashed in on the Brazilians' éclat. Tribesmen and tubers, so far as they were concerned, came from roughly the same neck of the woods.

There is some evidence that early imported tubers to Europe were a little bigger than those of wild plants, suggesting that the Native Americans had indeed brought *tuberosus* into cultivation. They offered it to the Pilgrim Fathers during their first starving winter in Massachusetts in 1620. In spite of their hunger, the Pilgrims, who knew very little about

Cyanara cardunculus and *Helianthus tuberosus*

farming or gardening, were deeply suspicious of the plants, like maize and *tuberosus*, offered to them out of the wilderness; they then learned out of necessity to appreciate their culinary value.

Conversely, when *tuberosus* came to Europe its popularity was great—everyone wanted to cultivate and consume the plant that was so easy to grow. In 1617 a Mr John Goodyer planted two small roots at Mapledurham in Hampshire; four years later he was stocking up the gardens of the rest of the county.

John Parkinson, in his 1629 *Paradisus*, described and illustrated the new vegetable (which he called "Jerusalem artichoke" and "potato of Canada") and spoke of it as a "dainty for a queen."

In early cooking recipes it was boiled and peeled, then sliced and stewed with butter, wine and spices. Or it was pie-baked with dates, ginger, marrow or raisins. Then a public reaction to the artichoke occurred: it tasted of soot, or of nothing at all; it made you fart; it was tolerable as a curiosity in a corner of the garden, but it was not worth growing as a field crop; it was fit only for pigs.

Tuberosus may not be to everyone's taste, but it is very nutritious. The tubers contain a sugar, inulin, and no potatoey starches or sucrose sugars, so they can be safely eaten by diabetics. Smoother, less knobbly tubers that are easier to peel have been developed—the old French variety, Fuseau, shaped like a spindle, is a popular cultivar. But it remains a minor garden vegetable, utterly eclipsed by its close relative, the annual sunflower, *H. annuus*, which is the world's third most important vegetable oil-producing plant and widely grown in the former USSR.

H. annuus originated, like *tuberosus*, in North America, but on the west coast. There is archaeological evidence that Native Americans were farming it from Canada to Mexico 2,000 years before the Europeans arrived. It can hybridize with *tuberosus*, producing fertile offspring: specialist breeders have used the less glamorous cousin to build resistance in *H.annuus* to several major diseases.

HELIANTHUS TUBEROSUS: JERUSALEM ARTICHOKE IN FLOWER

Dordogne, France

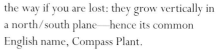

Lettuce

Lactuca sativa *of the* Daisy *family*

The world's most important salad plant probably descends from a tall, weedy, nasty-smelling, bitter-tasting, sow-thistle-like biennial herb called Prickly Lettuce, *Lactuca serriola*.

A southern, sun-living plant that probably originated on the Mediterranean rim, *serriola* has colonized vast areas of the northern temperate zone in the Old World and, post-Columbus, in the New. It likes waste and rocky ground, woodland clearings and rubbish tips and you can recognize it by its small, pale yellow, daisy-like flowers carried in late summer on top of 6ft-high stems, and its grayish, alternate, oblong leaves that (at the top of the stem and in the sunshine) can point you

the way if you are lost: they grow vertically in a north/south plane—hence its common English name, Compass Plant.

Garden lettuce, *sativa*, can interbreed with wild *serriola*, and with two other similar wild species of Mediterranean origin: *L. saligna*, Least Lettuce, which is smaller and slenderer and grows on bare grass or shingle, often near the sea; and *L. virosa*, Great or Poison Lettuce, which holds its leaves horizontally, and has blackish seeds.

Trying to sort out which is the ancestor of what is not easy. The best guess is that a fifth, probably extinct species hybridized with *serriola* to make *sativa*, or vice versa, or that *sativa* and *serriola* were both part of the same hybrid population that diverged at an early date: the one being selected for human cultivation, the other adapting to waste ground niches created by man.

It is thought that the earliest lettuces, like oats, radishes, leeks and beet, may well have been brought into cultivation "through the back door"—occurring as weeds in the first crops of emmer wheat and barley that were grown in the valleys of the Nile, Tigris and Euphrates.

They were probably first tolerated, then deliberately planted, more for the edible oil in their seeds than for their salad leaves, which

A Gardener Waters His Lettuces
c.2,494–2,345 B.C.

FIFTH DYNASTY

A master sketch for the unfinished decoration of the Tomb of Neferherenptah

would have been unpleasantly bitter. The "bitter herbs" that Jehovah told the Israelites to eat with roast lamb at the time of the Passover in Egypt (Exodus 12:8) may well have included leaves from these wild, or semi-wild plants that occur commonly throughout the Nile Delta and the Middle East.

Serriola lettuces—and garden lettuces—exude from their cut stems a white, milky, bitter-tasting latex which contains a narcotic substance akin to laudanum. If you chew enough lettuce before you go to bed, you are likely to sleep well.

For early civilisations in the Middle East, the latex seems to have had seminal associations: in ancient Egyptian mythology the plant was sacred to Min, goddess of fertility, and the God Seth is supposed to have become pregnant after eating lettuces over which Horus scattered his semen. From about 2,500 B.C. lettuces were used routinely as sacred offerings to Min and temple priests were banned from eating the plant.

The Egyptians used it in their herbal medicine, too, according to surviving texts: boiled in fat and mixed with date juice as a poultice; mixed with fresh beef, frankincense, juniper berries, bread, and beer and then strained and drunk for four days, for a stomach ache; boiled with oil, beer and other fermented plant juice, for a cough, and so on.

Egyptian tomb reliefs from the third millennium B.C. show tall, narrow-leaved plants like our Cos (or Roman) lettuces being tended by gardeners, and these may well have been among the first varieties of *sativa* to have been selected and grown in cultivated plots.

On the Mediterranean's northern shore in Greek classical times Theophrastus, in his

Enquiry into Plants, wrote of three lettuce cultivars, and other Greek writers mention the plant, which they called *tridax*, in medical and cooking contexts. Hippocrates, born on the island of Cos in 460 B.C., was well aware that lettuce juice was soporific. The Romans ate quantities of lettuce (especially after it was said to have done the emperor Augustus a lot of

RELIEF OF GOD MIN WITH A LETTUCE BEHIND HIM

Limestone
Ashmolean Museum
Oxford, U.K.

good), so that it eventually grew throughout their empire, even in Britain. They called it *lactuca*, from the *lac* (milk) in the latex.

In the first century A.D., Pliny the Elder knew of nine different varieties. They were loose-leaved and headless, but less latex-filled and therefore less bitter and narcotic, and able to be eaten fresh in salads. A common Roman practice was to blanch the lower leaves, and store them in jars of brine and vinegar.

The ancient world could never quite make up its mind about when exactly to eat the plant: at the beginning of a meal to stimulate the appetite, or at the end to induce sleep. In the first century A.D., Rufus of Ephesos declared that eating lettuce fogged the memory and prevented swift thought; a hundred years later Galen from Pergamon, the Greek dietician whose influence extended right down to the Middle Ages and beyond, ate lettuce last thing at night to stop the mental churning that prevented him from studying properly the next day.

Western Cos-type lettuces are thought to have arrived in China fairly late, between about A.D. 600 and 900. The Chinese already had their own native wild lettuce, *Lactuca indica*, a perennial with coarse, reddish, lanceolate leaves which they ate, and still eat, cooked. Celtuce or asparagus lettuce (*Lactuca sativa* var. *augustana*), increasingly popular in the West, was developed in China and brought to France in the nineteenth century by returning missionaries.

It is not known when hearted "cabbage" lettuces were first selected and grown. They are nowadays subdivided into "butterheads," with soft, round, overlapping leaves forming a heart, and "crispheads" with crisp leaves making a tight head (Iceberg is typical). The first definite evidence for them occurs in the sixteenth century, although they probably had existed for some time before that, especially on the European continent. Modern-looking butterhead lettuces are clearly shown in *Allegory of Summer*, by Lucas van Valkenborch, who painted in Flanders and died in 1597.

In 1614, Giacomo Castelvetro, an Italian exile in England wrote nostalgically of the summer lettuce salads he enjoyed in his native land. He described two types: *romana* [Cos] with long smooth leaves that gardeners in Italy tied tightly round a cane to blanch them "white as snow"; and *capucina*, crisp, white and sleep-inducing, with a solid heart which, cut into four parts, could be oiled, salted and peppered and roasted over a charcoal grill, then eaten, sprinkled with orange juice.

Lettuces were being grown in the New World within two years of Columbus' arrival. They particularly enjoyed the temperate sunshine of the North American west coast. There are wild lettuces native to the Americas—the Canadian lettuce, which looks like serriola with dandelion leaves—but they are bitter-tasting and more or less inedible. In the early 1900s Californian growers favoured the crisphead cultivars which were robust enough to withstand being ice-shipped long distances.

Today, with vacuum cooling and dry packing techniques, an ever-widening range of shapes and colors of this very variable plant is available to consumers all over the world.

LETTUCE LEAVES IN PURPLE WICKER, 1996 *(opposite)*
E.B. WATTS
Acrylic on paper
Private Collection

ALLEGORY OF SUMMER *(detail)*
LUCAS VAN VALCKENBORCH
1535–1597
Oil on canvas
Johnny Van Haeften Ltd London, U.K.

Black & capsicum pepper

Piper nigrum *of the* Pepper *family and*

Capsicum *of the* Nightshade *family*

Black pepper, one of the first spices ever to be farmed by man, originated in southern India. *Piper nigrum* is a perennial, tropical, tendriled vine whose dried fruits are sold all over the world today as peppercorns.

Wild plants can still be found growing in the Western Ghats, overlooking India's southwestern Malabar coast.

Dried peppercorns may seem to last forever in a pepperpot, but pepper seeds have an active life of only about seven days. So it is thought that, in pre-Christian times, the plant was spread clonally, by cuttings, from its center of origin in southern India, north to the Himalayas, and east to China and southeast Asia, where it discovered good habitats and eager appetites.

Spice grinding stones for pepper have been identified in Pakistan's Indus valley civilisation dating from about 2000 B.C. and there was a pepper trade in Egypt, Babylon and Greece from an early date. The Greeks already had a name for it in the fifth century B.C.: they called it *to peperi*, a name perhaps evolved from the ancient Sanskrit word for a dried fig, *pippali*. Imports, possibly stimulated by the Indian campaigns of Alexander the Great that took place either side of 330 B.C., came to Athens during the Hellenistic period, along with sesame oil and rice from the other side of India, the Gangetic plain. The Romans used pepper too—they called it *piper*.

When Marco Polo set out from Venice in 1271 on his twenty-four-year odyssey through Asia, an important trade in pepper was in existence, based mainly in Venice at one end and on the Malabar coast at the other. Arab sailing dhows or overland camel caravans came from India to Aden. Polo witnessed the trade there in person:

Aden is a great resort for merchants. In this port they transfer their goods to other small ships, which sail for seven days along a river.
At the end of this time they unload the goods and pack them on camels and carry them thus for about thirty days, after which they reach the river of Alexandria; and down this river they are easily transported to

Alexandria itself. This is the route from Aden by which the Saracens of Alexandria receive pepper and spices and precious wares.

From Alexandria, it was a fairly easy run across the Mediterranean to Genoa or Venice. Peppercorns were cheap in the East. Polo reported forty-three cartloads of 223 pounds, each being brought daily into the Great Khan's capital city of Kinsai (Hang-chau in eastern China). He saw pepper being grown "in great abundance in all the fields and woods" near

Pepper Harvest in Coilum, Southern India

Boucicaut Master

1390–1430

Vellum

Bibliothèque Nationale

Paris, France

Coilum in southern India. "It is gathered in the months of May, June and July. And I can tell you that the pepper trees are planted and watered and grown in cultivation." But it was a different story by the time it arrived in Europe. There it was like gold dust, counted out peppercorn by peppercorn. The medieval housewife kept the key of her spice cupboard carefully concealed about her person. This was not so much because her meat was off, more that in the middle ages, with the exception of breeding and draught stock, most animals were slaughtered in the autumn and hung up to cure for the lean winter months, and pepper from the Orient put some much needed pungency into the meat dishes.

In its fifteenth-century heyday, Venice ran a spice fleet of twenty great galleys, each capable of carrying 250 tons, and grew rich and powerful on the proceeds. Next it was Portugal's turn: Vasco da Gama discovered the eastern sea route to the Indies around the Cape of Good Hope, and Portuguese merchants sourced their spices direct in Goa and thereby cut out the Arab middlemen.

By 1523 the Germans were complaining that:

the King of Portugal, with spices under his control, has set prices as he will, because at no manner of dearness will they rest unsold among the Germans . . . The merchants moreover do not make everything dear at the same time. Now it may be saffron and cloves.

One year pepper and ginger,
another year nutmeg, and so on,
to the intent that their advantage
may not at once be apparent
to people.

Thirty years before, Columbus had sailed west, on behalf of Spain and its king and queen, Ferdinand and Isabella. The expedition's motives were, in part, altruistic: to roll back the infidel—Islam had just been evicted from Spanish soil—and to christianize the Orient.

But opening up a western trade route to the Spice Islands was the bigger lure. In the event Columbus found no Asians to christianize, no black pepper, and no great cities such as Marco Polo had described. He died in obscurity in 1506, but he did discover American Capsicum pepper, the most important spice plant of the twentieth century. Peter Martyr was tutor to the royal princes when Columbus came to the Spanish court at Barcelona in April 1493 with news of his discoveries. That spring and summer Martyr, fascinated by the New World, took the opportunity to cross-question crew members; in September he put down the first ever mention of capsicum peppers in any

language (in Latin, in fact) in his *De Orbe Novo*:

Something may be said about the pepper gathered in the islands . . . . but it is not pepper, though it has the same strength and flavor, and is just as much esteemed. The natives call it axi, it grows taller than a poppy. When it is used there is no need of Caucasian pepper.

PEPPER PLANT
SEVENTEENTH
CENTURY
British Library
London, U.K.

**TOMATOES AND
RELATED
VEGETABLES, 1986**
(opposite)
ELIZABETH RICE
Watercolor on paper
Private Collection

Capsicum peppers originated in the tropical Americas, but exactly where and when is uncertain; one theory—it is little more than a guess really—suggests a nuclear area in central Bolivia, bisected by the Río Grande.

Unlike black pepper (to which they are quite unrelated) the capsicums are great colonizers and hybridizers, their many, tough, long-lasting seeds being readily spread by birds. Up to thirty species have been identified, of which five have been domesticated.

In the wild, peppers range from the southern United States down across Central America to the Andean highlands of Bolivia and Peru and the low-lying rainforests of the

Amazon. Fruits of wild species tend to be bright red and pointing upward on bare, deciduous branches to advertise themselves to birds, while those of most domesticated cultivars, which occur in a variety of shapes and colors, hang down amid concealing leaves.

Outside the tropics, in temperate zones, peppers are mostly farmed as herbaceous annuals. The thirty-odd wild types identified by botanists can be more or less reduced to five core species, all of which have been brought into domestication.

Capsicum frutescens, a weedy, bushy shrub with greenish-white flowers and red pods pointing upward, originated in the tropics of

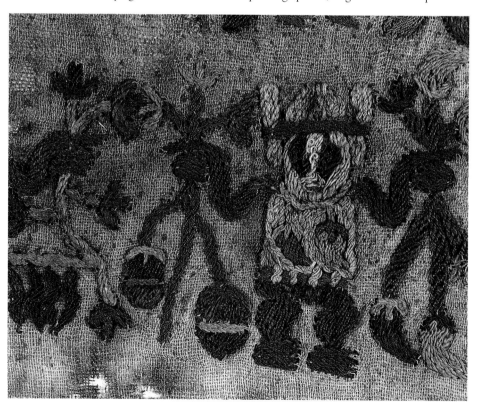

**FIGURE OF A MAN
HOLDING CHILI
PEPPERS**
NAZCA PERIOD
A.D. 400–600
Embroidery
*Phoebe Apperson Hearst
Museum of Anthropology
Berkeley, U.S.*

lowland South America. The cultivar derived from it, Tabasco, named after a Mexican town, makes the pungent sauce that we dribble onto oysters or Bloody Marys.

Capsicum baccatum, with brown or yellow spots on the white petals, and yellow anthers, is a native of Bolivia and likes subtropical conditions. It is not much grown outside South America.

Capsicum chinense is very like *frutescens* and was wrongly named in the eighteenth century; it is a native, in fact, of western Brazil.

Capsicum pubescens, the rocoto, is very distinct: it has large purple flowers and dark, rough seeds and thrives in the cool, humid highlands of the Andes and Mexico, where it is still grown. Fruits tend to be roundish; red, yellow or orange; and very hot. It was a favorite plant of the Incas, who made use of it in their religion and myths.

Capsicum annuum var. *annuum*, last of the five core species, is the world's most widely cultivated pepper. It is the source of most of the sweet pepper cultivars that we cut up for salads or eat as vegetables. It is also the variety of the hotter, sun-dried, chili and cayenne peppers, that are ground up into chili powder and paprika. The riper the fruit and more intense the sun, the more capsaicin acid is stored in the flesh and seeds, which are the hottest part of all.

The wild counterpart of *annuum* var. *annuum* (which denotes the domesticated varieties) is *C. annuum* var. *glabriusculum*, the Chillipiquin or Bird-pepper. It has white flowers, blue anthers, small red fruits and grows as a weed on roadsides, canyons and disturbed places from the southern U.S. to northern South America.

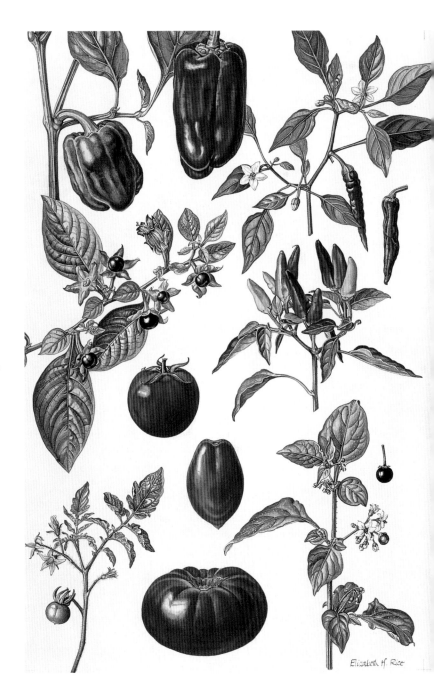

Elizabeth H. Rice

RED PEPPERS
(CAPSICUM OR
ANAHEIM CHILI),
1995 *(opposite)*
JESSICA TCHEREPNINE
Watercolor on paper
Private Collection

Peppers were grown and eaten by American Indians long before Columbus arrived and they were probably not that much different from the cultivars that we know today. Pepper seeds, most likely of *C. annuum,* have been found in human dung remains in the Tehuacan valley caves, 150 miles south of Mexico City, and have been dated to about 7,000 B.C. But the dung may have been left by hunter-gatherers rather than farmers.

Better evidence of early pepper farming comes from the 2,500-B.C. site of Huaca Prieta, in the Chicama valley of northern Peru, where whole peppers, not big, but clearly bigger than fruits of wild species, have been recovered. Here, Stone Age Indians practiced some of the earliest farming in the Americas—but we can not be certain that these peppers (*C. baccatum* and *frutescens*) were sown on purpose; they could have grown among staple Indian crops like maize and manioc as adventitious weeds.

One of the earliest known representations of peppers is carved on the Tello obelisk, now in the Archaeological Museum at Lima, and dated to between A.D. 800 and 1,000. This granite shaft, taller than a man, was found by a farmer in the early 1900s in temple ruins high up in the Peruvian Andes at the headwaters of the Amazon, and clearly shows a mythical creature holding in its claws the flowers, leaves and four pods of a *capsicum* plant.

Early eyewitness

HAND-COILED
POTTERY
AZTEC PERIOD
MEXICO
Museum für Volkerkunde,
Berlin, Germany
The bottom of the dishes
have been scored, which
suggests that they may
have been used for
grinding pepper

accounts by Spanish conquistadores and the Jesuit priests who accompanied them all confirm the importance in the Indian diet of what was called *chilli* by the Mexican Aztecs, *ají* by the West Indian islanders that Columbus encountered, and *uchu* by the Peruvian Incas. The colonists called the new plant *pimiento.*

Oviedo, a Spanish *caballero,* who arrived in Panama in 1513 and published a book about the New World in 1526, gives a typical account: "The Indians everywhere grow it in gardens and farms . . . they eat it continuously with almost all of their food." He claims that it was taken at an early date to Italy and Spain, where it was considered an excellent spice and better with meat and fish than "good black pepper."

Bartolemé de las Casas arrived as a soldier in the New World in 1502. Later he worked many years among the Indians as a Dominican friar, and became the first priest to be ordained in the New World. In his book *Historia de las Indias 1520–1561,* published long after his

Piper nigrum and *Capsicum*

death, he recorded three kinds of *ají* pepper used by the Indians as seasoning: one long, red and finger-shaped, another cherry-like and hotter (both of these he saw growing in Indian gardens), and a third wild variety —probably the bird-pepper, *C.* var. *glabriusculum*—with tiny red fruits.

Farther south, in Brazil, which was first colonized in 1507, Hans Stade, a Hessian, was held prisoner by Indians from 1547 to 1555. He recorded two colors of ripe pepper fruit: yellow and red:

When green it is as large as the haws that grow on hawthorns. It is a small shrub, about half a fathom high and has small leaves. It is full of peppers that burn the mouth. They pluck it when it becomes ripe, and they dry it in the sun.

Capsicum peppers, unlike their *Solanaceae* relatives, potatoes and tomatoes, which took centuries to be accepted by Europe, were a fairly immediate hit in the Old World. Ground down, they were a passable imitation of the hugely expensive black pepper—and their plants revelled in the Mediterranean sunshine. The first seeds may well have come back with Columbus. It was not long before they were being passed eastwards along the Portuguese trade routes from Lisbon via Brazil to Goa in India, where three species were recorded growing in 1542, and to the Portuguese colony of Macao in China, where they rapidly spread;

or westwards across the Pacific on the annual Spanish silver galleon that left Acapulco for Manila in the Philippines from 1565 onwards for 150 years, returning to Mexico laden with silks. They penetrated northern Europe from the Balkans, imported by Ottoman Turks, and at about the northern limit of their range they were given an enthusiastic welcome by the Hungarians, who became major producers of *capsicums* in Europe. The Hungarians were referring to them as *paprika* as early as 1569.

Today, it is the sweet *capsicums* that receive most attention from farmers and breeders, while the hot chili peppers remain much the same as they were when they livened up the food of the Stone Age Peruvian Indians. China is the biggest *capsicum* producer in Asia, Spain the biggest in Europe, and peppers from Mexico, where their story in part began, are exported all over the

Potato

Solanum tuberosum *of the* Nightshade *family*

If the potato (from the same family as Deadly Nightshade) had just been invented, it would be banned by the Food and Drug Administration. At ninety parts per million, it contains about one quarter of the concentration of the poisonous, bitter alkaloid, solanin, that is required to kill a human being. Left to go green in the light, its tubers become more toxic, which is why potatoes should always be stored in the dark and checked for proper color before cooking.

The potato grows wild in the American western mountains between forty-five degrees north and south, on the high spine that runs from Wyoming down through Mexico's Sierra Madre to the Chilean Andes.

Over two hundred wild tuber-bearing *Solanum* species have been identified by botanists, growing from sea level up to the snow line (mostly, they prefer the South American highlands, where the days are hot and the nights are bitter cold). The majority have deep eyes, knobbly tubers and high alkaloid contents. Others have long underground rhizomes that grow tubers at long distances from the parent, or prostrate leaves like the dwarf, stalkless *Solanum demissum*, which grows in the pine forests of Mexico's Sierra Madre where butterflies overwinter.

Solanum jusepczukii, the highest food plant in the world, shrugs off the icy night winds of the Peruvian high Andes at 14,763ft. It can tolerate up to eight degrees of frost. Tuber colors vary enormously: red, yellow, white, purple, blue,

even black. You can still buy strange wildings gathered by Indians in South American markets; some have Spanish names (*papa amarilla*, a yellow potato with a waxy texture, for example, or the *ulluco*, thumb-shaped and yellow-green-fleshed and highly prized) and often cost more than their cultivated cousins.

With so many possible hybridizing species to choose from, it is little wonder that botanists are unable to decide exactly how our modern *tuberosum* potato descends. But they agree, on the whole, about where the first edible potatoes grew and where and when they were cultivated.

In Marxist Russia, the potato was a crucial crop: it filled vodka bottles and fed the proletariat. For seven years from 1925, a Russian research team scoured the 4,000-mile length of the Andes for *Solanum* specimens; the project was the brainchild of the pioneering geneticist, N.J. Vavilov, who later disappeared in the Gulag, a victim of Stalin's purge of the botanists after World War II. The conclusion of their research was that the first edible potatoes grew wild in the Andean highlands at about the fifteenth parallel (the area round La Paz and Lake Titicaca), and spread north and south from there.

What probably occurred was this. Around 5,000 B.C. (more or less when the llama began to be used by man for pack-carrying, and the alpaca for wool), primitive hunter gatherers moved west out of the Amazon jungle and up onto the high, windswept, treeless plateau around Lake Titicaca on the Peru/Bolivia border– the same area, coincidentally, in which the Inca originated. Here they found and ate mutant wild potato tubers less bitter, and therefore less toxic, than previously encountered (mutants occur in wild plants about one in 50,000 times).

Not burdened by notions of tidiness, they threw their leftovers onto heaps outside their huts, where the piles of household waste and animal dung proved fertile nursery beds for tubers, which became gardened, as it were, by mistake. It was a short step, thence, to purposeful farming. The Indians had found a way to exist on the *altiplano*.

Potato provided a good starchy, vitamin-rich diet, with some protein, and grew at altitudes impossible for maize. It could be stored, too, for lean times (*chuño*, sliced potato, dried out in the cold winds, is still eaten all over South America). Carried down by llama to the arid Pacific coast, where it was too hot for the potato to grow, it could be bartered for maize, clothing and pottery.

Archaeological traces of potato have been found in Chilca canyon south of Lima dating from 4,000 B.C. and Peruvian coastal burial pots made in the form of potatoes, with deep-

cut eyes, have survived from about A.D. 1000, suggesting that the plant was cultivated in the first millennium A.D., if not long before.

In 1532, when Francisco Pizarro and his small band of men and horses kidnapped the Inca ruler Atahuallpa, he found himself in control of a huge, well-adminstered country twice the size of Spain. In one sense, the Indians were still in the Stone Age: they had no knowledge of iron, the wheel or the written word; they had never seen a cow, horse, sheep or goat; for protein, they ate bugs and guinea-pigs. But in another sense their culture, based on sophisticated agrarian techniques, was highly developed and organized. Maize grew on the lower, arid ground along the Pacific coast, and in the Andean valleys. Higher in the mountains, gangs of workmen (fed on maize and *chuño*) had cut terraces and built aqueducts for growing potatoes.

The variable cultivar that the Incas grew (they called it *Papa*) had been improved by centuries of selection even before the Spanish arrived. It was very similar to that which is still widely grown in the Andes from Colombia to northern Argentina: a fair weather plant, with knobbly tubers, deep-set eyes, thin stems and a dense, bushy habit. Its flowers are white, magenta or purple. It

RUSSIAN PEASANT WITH VODKA BOTTLE
NATALJA SERGEEVNA GONCHAROVA
1881–1962
Victoria & Albert Museum London, U.K.

**THE POTATO EATERS,
1885**

VINCENT VAN GOGH

1853–1890

Oil on canvas

Rijksmuseum, Amsterdam

The Netherlands

likes a humid atmosphere, but dislikes bad drainage, and grows best in the tropical Andes at heights between 7,874 and 12,795ft. Too low down, and it is killed by blight; too high up and the frost gets it (which recalls the varieties of the Scottish east coast, where the best seed potatoes can be found). It is a short-day plant, stimulated to grow best when the hours of daylight are fewer than twelve. Two or more crops of it a year can be grown, but the farmers are lucky to recover one harvest out of five unaffected by frost—there is no summer or winter in those latitudes, just hot days and cold nights in the mountains. This cultivar's taxonomic name is *S. tuberosum* subspecies *andigenum* (or the Andigena Group, to embrace its many varieties).

Who first introduced the potato to Europe and when? It is more or less certain, judging by early descriptions and illustrations in herbals — in particular, a 1588 aquarelle (watercolor) of a plant given to the French scientific botanist De l'Écluse, and a very precise description by him in his *Historia* of 1601, that it was this cultivar that was imported to Europe in the sixteenth century.

The first European recorded as seeing a

potato was Juan de Castellanos. He was a member of a Spanish raiding party that, early in 1537, hacked its way through the dense tropical forests of the Magdalena valley in Colombia's northern Andes. On the high plateau to the east of the river, the raiders came upon an Indian village, whose inhabitants fled in panic. Inside their huts the Spaniards found maize, beans and what Castellanos called "*turmas de tierra*" or truffles. They were round or elongated, egg-sized, and purple, white or yellow, and came, he said, from plants with

scanty flowers of a dull purple color and floury roots of a good flavor, a gift very acceptable to Indians and a dainty dish even for Spaniards.

A few months later, the same expedition captured Bogota from the Chibcha Indians. It was noted that the truffle (potato) was a staple food of the highlanders, and yielded good crops.

For centuries it was believed that the first potatoes were brought back from the Elizabethan colony of Virginia. Had not John Gerard written so in his *Herball*, first published in 1597? Gerard was excited by the potato—he claims he grew it in his Holborn garden in the 1590s. He pictured himself on the *Herball*'s frontispiece holding the new plant. But, as usual, the London barber-surgeon and plagiarist got into a muddle; the potatoes he grew in his garden, far from being North American in origin, were probably taken on as cooks' stores in the Caribbean in 1586, by the very ship (it was Sir Francis Drake's) that evacuated back to Plymouth most of Raleigh's

second expedition to Virginia.

All the evidence suggests that the first tubers were imported by returning Spaniards in the late 1560s. Brought down the newly built road from the Bogota potato fields and embarked at Cartagena on the Caribbean coast of what is now Colombia (the so-called Spanish Main), they were then unloaded where Spanish ships from the New World commonly discharged their cargo—up the Guadalquivir

INCAS HARVESTING POTATOES, c.1565
FELIPE GUAMAN POMA
Biblioteca Real
Copenhagen, Denmark

where it was known as *cantoufle* or simply *truffe*—gardeners were excited by its potential as a cultivated truffle.

It was grown in the Low Countries by the 1580s and in the 1590s reached England (possibly a separate introduction of *andigenum,* direct from the New World). Raleigh may well have grown it on his Irish estate in Co Cork, where, according to legend, his gardener sent not the tubers, but the green fruit berries up to the kitchen for cooking.

In 1621, the potato sailed back across the Atlantic with the Pilgrim Fathers to New England, where it was previously unknown.

From an early date, the Spanish conquistadors recognized the potato's potential: they fed it to their slave workers in the Peruvian silver mines at Potosi. But it took a very long time indeed to catch on as the staple food of the European working class.

In 1664, John Forster of Buckinghamshire published his *England's Happiness Increased, or a Sure and Easy Remedy Against all Succeeding Dear Years* (by a plantation of the roots called potatoes) but with little effect. Consumers—the rural poor of Protestant northern Europe especially—were deeply suspicious. It reminded them of Deadly Nightshade and Bittersweet. Did it not cause leprosy? Had it ever been recommended by the Bible? Was it not a Catholic plant, a creation of the Great Satan? It was fit, perhaps, for pigs. At Lewes, Sussex, in about 1765, an election slogan ran:

No Potatoes. No Popery.

A nineteenth-century Irish variety was called The Protestant, because "we boil the devil out." Seventeenth- and eighteenth-century northern European still life paintings

river at Seville. The 1573 accounts of the city's La Sangre hospital, includes the first known mention of the potato in Europe, in a list of vegetables bought in as winter stores.

Certainty, however, is elusive: the sweet potato, *Ipomaea batatas*, discovered by Columbus on Haiti, was also being imported from the Carribean during the sixteenth century, and from the early lists and descriptions one is never quite sure which variety is which.

From Spain, the potato travelled to Italy where it was called *tartufflo*, and to France,

Solanum tuberosum

of vegetable stalls and markets never feature *andigenum*.

There was another, more practical drawback with *andigenum*: it was (and is) a short-day plant. In Europe it took nearly two centuries of selective breeding, from the first few imports, for the potato to do a genetic somersault, and flower earlier as the summer days of higher latitudes lengthened, well before the killing frosts of autumn. The first imports grew long, sprawly stems during the summer, but tubered only in November, if at all.

When and by whom the potato was introduced to Ireland, and where it immediately flourished, is not known. One legend believes Raleigh was responsible, another that it was washed ashore with ship's stores from a wreck, possibly of the Armada.

It was welcomed by the Irish Catholic peasants as god sent. Their misery and degradation in the sixteenth and seventeenth centuries can hardly be overstated. Chilling, firsthand accounts by English militiamen have come down to us describing how, on a regular basis, crops and homes were burnt, and men, women and children randomly hunted down and killed in a policy of what would now be called ethnic cleansing.

The potato, when it arrived, possessed two advantages: it grew well in Ireland's moist, wet, relatively frost-free climate in the south and west, and it was difficult for marauding English troops to find and destroy. Potatoes can survive in store, if properly covered, drained and ventilated, for up to a year, and the Irish cottiers became adept at concealing potato-clamps, covered with ferns and turves, in the wilderness of the bogs. Their system of "lazybed" cultivation involved lifting only a proportion of the season's

PIZARRO AND HIS MEN SEIZE ATAHUALPA, 1532
THEODOR DE BRY
Private Collection

crop and leaving the rest in the ground to overwinter as seed. Soldiers, to extirpate a crop, would have to dig over an entire field.

During the twenty years of rebellion and destruction sparked off by the massacre of Protestant colonists in Ulster in October 1641, it was the potato, a staple food—indeed, by now their only food—that saved the Irish peasantry from utter annihilation.

By about 1800, in the rest of Europe earlier-maturing cultivars had been developed and knobbly *andigenum* was merging into smooth *tuberosum*. The potato's truffle, bourgeois image had long since died; its excellent value as a cheap subsistence diet for the proletariat was beginning to be recognized.

In 1771 an official enquiry by the French Medical Faculty decided it was healthy and wholesome and in 1793 a decree of the Commune ordered a census to be taken of Paris luxury gardens, so that potatoes could be

from France. The disease first appeared on the Isle of Wight in August and wreaked havoc among English potatoes.

Ireland was infected in September, with terrible results. The Irish tubers were almost exclusively of the late, Lumper variety; that autumn they either rotted in the ground, or turned the potato clamps into stinking pools. Most of the crop was lost in 1845, all of it in 1846. Europe had known nothing like it since the Black Death. On 3rd August 1846, a Catholic priest, Father Mathew, traveled to Cork from Dublin. He later wrote:

I beheld with sorrow one wide waste of putrefying vegetation. In many places the wretched people were seated on the fences of their gardens, wringing their hands, and wailing bitterly the destruction that had left them foodless.

Starvation stalked the land. Typhus, cholera, dysentery and scurvy (purpura in its lethal form)—the Irish obtained their vitamin C from potatoes—were in grim attendance. Contemporary accounts tell of corpses left to lie in roadside ditches and dogs fighting over the remains. Aid from the central English Government came too little and too late. The infamous Gregory clause in the 1847 Poor Relief (Ireland) Act denied aid to anyone who leased or owned more than one sixth of an acre: the poor, in order to qualify, had to give up their potato plots.

RALEIGH SUPERVISING THE FIRST POTATO PLANTING IN IRELAND
UNKNOWN ARTIST
Engraving after Daniel Maclise from
Reliques of Father Prout *by Francis Sylvester*

planted. The King's Jardin de Tuileries, avenues included, became a huge potato patch.

In 1845, the year the potato Murrain devastated European potato fields from Poland to the Atlantic. *The Times* reported with alarm that the two main meals of an English worker's day consisted exclusively of potatoes; an alarm all the greater if the writer had known that the European potato originated from the tiny genetic base of the first few sixteenth-century *andigenum* imports, themselves highly susceptible to blight.

During that summer of 1845, spores of the fungus, *Phytopthera infestans* (the causal agent of the disease was identified a year later by Reverend M.J. Berkeley, a Northamptonshire parson) were windblown across the Channel

Solanum tuberosum

It has been estimated that in the five years of the Great Famine from 1845, out of a national Irish population of about eight million, over one and half million died, and a million more emigrated, many to America.

In the second half of the nineteenth century, in spite of *Phytopthera infestans*, the potato carried all before it. What the English call "chips" and Americans "french fries" did indeed originate in France. Sickle-shaped and known as *pommes Pont Neuf*, they were sold on the boulevards of *fin-de-siècle* Paris by street vendors. They traveled to England in the 1870s and to America soon afterwards. A 1878 cookbook that was published in New York and entitled *Practical Cooking and Dinner Going* by Mary F. Henderson, called them Saratoga potatoes.

American "chips" and the English "crisps" were, it is claimed, invented in the U.S. at much the same time by George Crum, chef at Moon's Lake House, Saratoga Springs, New York. The story goes that a diner kept sending back his french fries, complaining they were too thick. An exasperated Crum cut a potato into wafer-thin slices, fried them, and sent them back to, one hopes, a standing ovation. Crum had invented an industry now worth over $5 billion a year in the U.S. alone; potato chips account for nearly half the salty, packeted snacks eaten by Americans every year.

In Britain in the twentieth century, potatoes saw us through two world wars; they were our principal source of vitamin C, for troops and civilians alike. In 1916, when there was a partial crop failure at home, scurvy broke out in the army and in the factories.

Out of a total world roots-and-tubers production of six hundred million tons in

1998, the potato accounted for nearly half (278 million), far more than cassava (161 million) and sweet potato (118 million). China was the largest producer, with forty-one million tons. Other major growers included the Russian Federation, the U.S., Poland, India and the Ukraine. Ireland grew just under half a million tons.

THE POTATO FAMINE, *c.1846*

ARTIST UNKNOWN

A peasant contemplates the wretched crop of potatoes on which he and his family expected to live

Eggplant

Solanum melongena *of the* Nightshade *family*

The eggplant (also called aubergine, melongene, Jew's apple, mad apple, and brinjal) is the only edible member of the nightshade family, comprising seventy-five genera and over 2000 species, that did not originate in the New World. Our native version, the solanaceous Deadly Nightshade (*Atropa belladonna*) is not, of course, on the menu. Just two or three of its succulent black berries can kill a child—which may explain why aubergines, like potatoes, were heartily mistrusted by northern Europeans until the seventeenth century.

Nikolai Vavilov, the Soviet geneticist who scoured the globe between the Wars for new plants to feed the Russian Revolution, confirmed India as the center of origin of the eggplant. Alphonse de Candolle had already suggested the subcontinent in his *Origine des Plantes Cultivées,* published in 1882, on the basis of the number of names for eggplant that turn up in ancient Sanskrit, Bengali and Hindustani: *varrta, bong, bartakon, mahoti, bungan*. "It cannot be doubted," he wrote, "that the species has been known in India from a very remote epoch."

Today, botanists accept that the wild eggplant (*Solanum melongena* var. *insanum*— Linnaeus called it *incanum*), which grows on dry hillsides in India, is the protoparent from which all our modern eggplant cultivars derive. It is a smallish perennial shrub, heavily armed with prickles, and has very bitter, yellow when ripe fruits. In India, it is self-pollinating, and very variable. Other associated, weedy, perennial, very primitive

types, with small, egg-like fruits of variable shape and color, have been gathered and eaten for centuries as poor-man's food by villagers in the tropics and subtropics of Asia, from western India to Thailand. Over the years, the spines and bitterness of the wild plants have been bred out and fruit sizes have improved.

Our inheritance is a delicious fruit that, treated as a vegetable, can be boiled whole, or cut into strips and fried, or stuffed with small pieces of meat and baked in an oven. In Greece it is the base for moussaka. In France it is mixed with courgettes, tomatoes, peppers and garlic to make a ratatouille; in Sicily with capers, celery, olives and tomato sauce to make caponata. In Trinidad its fritters are called "baigani." Although it tastes pretty good, it does not, in fact, have much nutritional value: the fruits are more than ninety percent water.

The first record of eggplant cultivation comes from China in the fifth century B.C., though it was probably being gardened in India before then. None of the Greek or Roman gardening writers mention it, nor is there sign of it in Classical Mediterranean art.

It emerged from Asia with Islam. Within a century of the prophet Muhammad's burial at Medina in 632, Moslem hordes of the Ummayad Caliphate had swept through Egypt, and along the coast of North Africa to Spain, thence to Sicily and parts of the Languedoc. In their conquering progress they ripped out vineyards, anathematised by the prophet, and planted fruit and vegetables familiar from the East instead: lemons, limes and oranges from China and Indonesia, carrots from Afghanistan, eggplants from India.

Melanzana fructu pallido.

195

RATATOUILLE, 1954

SIR CEDRIC MORRIS

1889–1982

Oil on canvas

Private Collection

The eggplant's first contact with European soil was probably in Spain, in the eighth century. Spain was hot enough for them to thrive out of doors, in gardens or as a farm crop, as they like hot, humid growing conditions with temperatures above 77°F. They failed to penetrate the cooler parts of northern Europe for many centuries, even today they are only grown in countries like Britain and the Netherlands on a small scale, under glass.

Their membership of the Nightshade family did not help their popularity: Moors and goats might eat them and survive, it was rumoured, but they killed Christians stone dead, or, at best, sent them mad.

There was knowledge of them in England in John Gerard's day (his *Herball* came out in 1597); he wrote of sowing what he called "madde apples" on dung-heaps and covering the plants with sailcloth to make them germinate. He acknowledged that they were eaten in Spain and North Africa, but added this solemn health warning:

But I rather wish English men to content themselves with the meat and sauces of our owne country, than with fruit and sauce eaten with such peril; for doubtless these Apples have a mischievous qualitie, the use whereof is utterly to be forsaken....it is therefore better to esteem this plant and have it in the garden for your pleasure and the rarenesse thereof, than for any virtue or good qualites yet knowne.

A generation later, John Parkinson could not see what all the fuss was about. In his *Theatrum Botanicum* he noted that their English name was "'madde apples,' but many doe much marveile why they should be so called, seeing none have been knowne to receive any harme by eating of them." Parkinson warned that it was best to boil them in vinegar first, otherwise one risked a catalog of horrors: leprosy, piles, stinking breath, obstructions in the liver and spleen, complexion change into a "foule black and yellow colour."

Gerard's and Parkinson's plants were probably of the type that bore small, white, ovoid fruits: hence their early name, eggplants. In Germany, the *Hortus Eystettensis*, the garden book of the Prince Bishop of Eichstatt in Bavaria, published in 1613, featured a purple-fruited plant. It is the earliest known colored illustration of an eggplant.

Eggplants rarely feature in "still lives" until at least the seventeenth century. An exception is *Summer* painted in 1563 by Giuseppe Arcimboldo, the Italian mannerist painter. He delighted in using strange plants: corn and marrows recently arrived from the New World, eggplants that the Moors had grown in Spain.

Gerard's "madde apple" comes from the early Italian *melazana*; the French word *aubergine* comes from the Spanish *berengena*, itself a corruption of the Arabic *al-badingan* and the ancient Hindustani word, *bungan*, is audible in the Arabic: one can trace the westward and northern movement of the Indian eggplant in the echoes of men's speech.

Today, eggplants are grown in the humid tropics and subtropics right round the world, from the West Indies to the Philippines. In India, and Africa, south of the Sahara they remain an important part of the diet of the poor. The Japanese love eggplants and, with the Indians, have researched new cultivars

with good heterosis. Modern hybrid fruits can be oval, pear-shaped or spherical, and dark purple, yellowish green or white. They can weigh up to 18oz and, grown as annuals in the right environment, are ready for harvest four to six months after sowing. In the last thirty years the Indian fruit that was once thought lethal to Christians has become a regular item in the supermarket carts all around the world.

SUMMER, 1563
GIUSEPPE
ARCIMBOLDO
1527–1593
Oil on canvas
Kunsthistorisches Museum
Vienna, Austria

Tomato *Lycopersicum esculentum of the* Nightshade *family*

The first tomatoes, like potatoes (they are both members of the Nightshade family), evolved in prehistoric times on the arid west coast of South America. Potatoes began on the high Peruvian plateau round Lake Titicaca where the days are hot and the nights are freezing cold. For tomatoes, though, the warmer lowlands beckoned. They probably made their first home where they still grow—along the dry banks of rivers that flow west between the Peruvian Andes and the Pacific.

CHARLES DARWIN, PACING AN ELEPHANT TORTOISE
MEREDITH NUGENT
1830s

Here, during the growing season, the only moisture is from thick mists and temperatures are moderate, ranging between 59°F and 66°F, day or night. It is a perfect habitat for tomatoes that thrive on fine spray irrigation but hate their roots being waterlogged and are killed outright by frost.

Nine different species of wild tomatoes have been identified by botantists in Ecuador and Peru. All have yellow flowers, and two species bear colored fruit; the rest are green-fruited. A tenth species, *Lycopersicum cheesemanii*, grows close to the high tide mark in the Galapagos Islands, six hundred miles to the west. It is tolerant to salt and self-fertile, and has orange, yellow, sometimes even purple, fruit. Long isolation on an archipelago has turned it rather odd. It can be irrigated with seawater—a genetic trait which has not gone un-noticed by plant breeders. On the other hand, its seeds must be digested and voided by giant turtles—and only giant turtles—before they will germinate. The turtles are slow-movers, but then so are their digestions: the seeds become widely dispersed along the shoreline.

But it is the two species of color-fruited tomato on the mainland, *L. pimpinellifolium* and *L. esculentum* subsp. *cerasiforme*, that are responsible for our modern tomato. *Cerasiforme*, the cherry tomato, has played the major role. A short-lived perennial plant, it is able to pollinate itself and produce flowers and fruit in

DARWIN TESTING THE SPEED OF AN ELEPHANT TORTOISE (GALAPAGOS ISLANDS)

five months in the tropics. Its fruits are small—about one inch in diameter—and colored red or yellow, sometimes even a translucent white. Their taste is sharp and acidic, but not unpleasant. The plant is an aggressive coloniser, with a sprawling habit, and turns up frequently as a weed on cultivated ground in Central and South America.

The early Peruvian Indians seem to have ignored it. No word for it survives in their languages, nor any trace on their early pottery or textiles. Perhaps they picked and ate the fruits wild as they passed. No attempt at domestication seems to have been made at a time when maize, potatoes and cassava were being cultivated. But slowly, over the centuries, its seeds were dispersed by birds and animals and *Cerasiforme* spread 2,000 miles north from its evolutionary centre in Peru, to Central America and Mexico. It was here, archaeologists believe, in the Veracruz/Puebla region on the Gulf of Mexico's western shore, that Indians, sometime before A.D. 500, first cultivated, and improved, the hitherto unconsidered weed.

When Cortez began his two-year conquest of Mexico in 1519, he found the Aztecs growing and eating a fruit they called *tomatl*. It was bigger than the wild cherry tomato, coloured yellow (less commonly red), and tended to be ridged. This was the cultigen, if descriptions and illustrations in early herbals are anything to go by, that, along with other novelties like maize, potatoes and eggplants, was being shipped back to the Old World in the sixteenth century, probably in the holds of Spanish ships on the silver route from the Gulf of Mexico to Seville.

From Spain the *tomatl* (called *tomate* by the Spanish) travelled to Italy, perhaps via Naples which came under Spanish rule in 1522 (today, the countryside round Pompeii and Vesuvius is abundant with sun-enriched cherry tomatoes that are hung in Italian kitchens to dry). In 1544, at Venice, Pier Andrea Mattioli published a commentary on the first-century A.D. herbal of Dioscorides. He wrote:

Another kind of mandrake has been brought to Italy in our time, flattened...and segmented, green at first and when ripe of a golden color, which is eaten in the same manner as the eggplant —fried in oil with salt and pepper.

This is the first mention of the tomato in Europe, and the first hint that something might be wrong. Mandrakes, native to the Mediterranean, were fearsome plants, with more than a touch of magic: their poisonous roots resembled human limbs and they were commonly supposed to shriek when pulled up. A second, 1554 edition of Mattioli's herbal added that the plant had red fruits as well as yellow and he gave the Latin name, *mala aurea* or "golden apple" to the plant and the Italian word, *pomodoro*, which it still bears to this day.

Before the end of the sixteenth century, botanists had spotted its kinship with the dangerous nightshade (*Solanaceae*) family, and called it "wolf peach"—*Solanum lycopersicum* (later changed by Carl Linnaeus in his eighteenth-century binomial system to

Lycopersicum esculentum). Herbalists and consumers throughout Europe began to regard it with extreme suspicion. It might not kill you outright, the rumor went, but it had side effects, of which probably the least unpleasant were aphrodisiac.

An early Italian name for the tomato was *pomum amoris*, which was later adopted by the French to become *pomme d'amour*. A drawing, found in an Italian herbal later in the century, carried the following legend:

If I should eat of this fruit, cut in slices in a pan with butter and oil, it would be injurious and harmful to me.

In 1574 the highly influential herbalist from the Low Countries, Rembert Dodoens, gave tomatoes a resounding thumbs-down that came to be echoed in succeeding herbals down the centuries: "[They] are eaten by some prepared and cooked with pepper, salt and oil. They offer the body very little nourishment and that unwholesome."

John Gerard, the London barber-surgeon and shameless plagiarizer of Dodoens, described "love apples" in his 1597 herbal (the tomato's first mention in English): "In Spaine and those hot regions they used to eat [them] prepared and boil'd with pepper, salt and oil; but they yield very little nourishment to the body and the same naught and corrupt."

John Parkinson, in his *Paradisi in sole Paradisus Terrestris* (1629), is no more encouraging: "[they are] of a faire pale reddish color, or somewhat deeper, like unto an Orenge, full of a slimie juice and waterie pulp." For three hundred years the

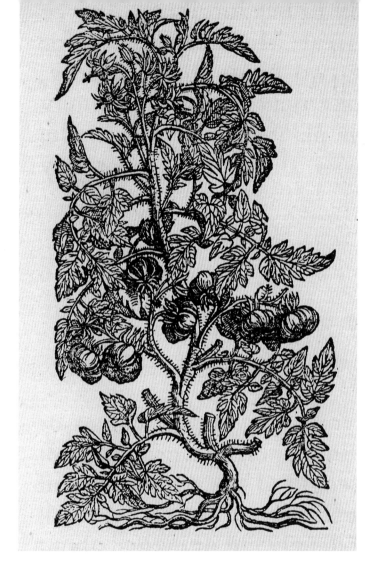

same prejudice persisted. Eighteenth- and even nineteenth-century herbalists insisted that the tomato was bad for you: it upset the stomach and caused faintness and apoplexy, or brought on colic or diarrhea.

In the teeth of such dispraise, it is hardly surprising that in Europe for many years it was grown only as an ornamental in the gardens of the rich: an indigestible curiosity. It never

LYCOPERSICUM ESCULENTUM **"APPLE OF LOVE" OR TOMATO, 1636**
JOHN GERARD
From the Historie of Plants *(1636 edition)*

features in paintings of fruit and vegetable markets before about 1800.

Gradually, however, the tide began to turn, not least in America. Thomas Jefferson, statesman and innovator, grew tomatoes for eating in his Monticello garden in Virginia in the 1780s; he called them "*tomatas,*" as did Dickens in *Pickwick Papers*. Records of the Philadelphia market show that they were being sold to French immigrants in the same decade. In 1820, Robert Gibbon Johnson, a rich, eccentric tomato convert, announced that he would eat, at noon, in public, a basket of tomatoes grown in his garden on the steps of the courthouse of Salem, New Jersey. A crowd

turned up to watch him die. His celebrated survival did wonders for the tomato's reputation, as, too, did the new varieties being developed by seedsmen.

By 1842, the *American Cultivator* magazine was reporting:

*Everybody cultivates the tomato
and everyone who has not
deliberately made up his mind to
be ranked among the nobodies
has learned to eat it.*

Lycopersicum esculentum

In 1870 a new variety, Paragon, bred in Ohio, was touted as "the first perfectly smooth, deep red tomato ever offered to the American People." In the same year in France, Alexandre Dumas died and, in his posthumously-published *Grande Dictionnaire de Cuisine*, he wrote of the tomato as a "fruit which comes to us from the people of the south, who treat it with honor. Its flesh is eaten in purée form and its sweet juice is used in seasoning." In America and elsewhere, around the time when Dumas was writing, the fashion seems to have been to cook it to death, for three hours or more, to get rid of the taste; only in more recent years has it become established as a fresh ingredient of salads or sandwiches.

In the twentieth century, and particularly since the 1940s, the tomato has been one of the most intensively researched, and culturally improved, of all our vegetables (In strict botanical terms, Dumas was correct: it is a fruit or berry, for it develops from a fertilized ovary; but in practice, by cooks and gardeners, it is treated as a vegetable). Cultivars have been developed to resist the many pests and diseases which tomatoes are heir to, or to fruit early or late or simultaneously, or to stop growing at a certain stage (the so-called determinate varieties), or to grow in colder latitudes; and so on. In the last decade the stakes have been vastly raised by the new GM technology—the so-called Flavr Savr tomato became the first GM whole food, in 1987, to go on the market in the U.S., with its ripening gene switched off so that it would remain firm after harvesting.

Today, tomatoes are grown all round the world, from the tropics to within a few degrees of the poles. They are a great favorite with home gardeners, and in areas like Turkey and California they are grown in huge fields of 494 acres or more, in straight, mechanically-harvested lines. Like their ancestors, the wild tomatoes of Peru, they thrive in sun and well-drained soil. They are a major source of vitamins, particularly vitamins A and C—one medium-sized tomato will provide about half the daily requirement of vitamin C for an adult. In the U.S., they are made into ketchup, purée and soup (Joseph Campbell began canning tomatoes in New Jersey in 1869). In Italy, where the best and tastiest tomatoes still come from, they have inspired a wonderful national cuisine. In northern Europe they sell truckloads of greenhouses and heating equipment. In China (the world's largest grower ahead of America, producing sixteen million tons in 1998, and rising) they are put

CAMPBELL'S
TOMATO SOUP
POSTER, 1949
U.S.

Leek

Allium porrum *of the* Lily *family*

The *Allium* genus, that includes our cultivated leeks, garlic and onions, probably originated long before historic time somewhere in the harsh, desolate steppes of central Asia, between the Caucasus and the Himalayas.

Over millennia it speciated outwards from its center of origin: modern botany has identified over six hundred species in a genus that ranges over most of the northern temperate zone of the Old World, from North Africa to the China seas.

There are some *alliums* native to North America, but almost all have a chromosome number of seven, and Old World species, which includes all our important garden cultivars, have a basic number of eight. This indicates an evolutionary separation in far off geological time, when North America was still a part of the northern supercontinent, Laurasia, and before she drifted away, with her cargo of primitive plants, to the other side of the Atlantic.

An *allium* that found a niche in the Old World—generally considered the immediate ancestor of our cultivated leek—is the wild leek or Great Round-headed Garlic, *Allium ampeloprasum*. You can find it growing all round the Mediterranean rim, especially in North Africa, and on into Asia as far as the Hindu Kush. It prefers hot, dry, even desert habitats of rock or sand (although it has pushed up into northern Europe and is even found, rarely, in Britain). A perennial, very variable plant with a pungent garlicky smell, it grows a stout stem up to 6½ft high, leafy to the middle, that carries a large globular head of white, purple, pink or red flowers. The leaves are flat and rough at the edges and the bulb at the base is surrounded by little yellowish bulbils. A cultivated form of the plant—Great-headed Garlic—is still grown on a small scale in Mediterranean gardens for its bulb, which has a mild, oniony-garlicky flavor.

Root and leaf vegetables like leeks do not oblige plant historians by surviving in archaeological contexts. The earliest evidence of regular human leek-eating—and by implication domestication—comes from a literary source: three cuneiform tablets in the Babylonian collection at Yale University dated to the Old Babylonian Period (*c.*1,700 B.C.), listing the earliest-known recipes in the history of cooking. The tablets were acquired from a dealer in 1933, but the style, script and vocabulary indicate southern Mesopotamia, where we know that other plants like watermelon, melon, garlic, onions and lettuce were grown in food gardens from at least the second millennium B.C.

The tablets contain about 375 lines of text, some of it too damaged to decipher in full, and thirty-five recipes, all for boiled dishes (*bouillons*) and some of them very detailed. A favorite ingredient in the *bouillons*, along with fresh fat of lamb, is a mixture of crushed leek and garlic. One, typical recipe is for boiled pigeon:

Split the pigeon in two. You need also some other meat. Place in water. Add fat, salt as you wish, cereal cake crumbed, onion and samidhu [another kind of allium*]; leek and garlic and aromatic herbs earlier steeped in milk.*

These early leeks may have resembled *kurrat* leeks, a variety still widely grown in the Middle East today for its narrow green leaves, which are chopped up fresh and used like chives. *Kurrats* (Arabic for leeks) are smaller and slenderer than var. *porrum*, and have a more pronounced bulb.

Remains of leeks, preserved in the extreme aridity of the tombs, have turned up in second-millennium-B.C. pharaonic Egypt, and leek-like plants occur in Middle Kingdom (2,133–1,786 B.C.) paintings. They were among the vegetables left behind in Egypt that the Jews, bored with their manna diet, longed for during their long march Exodus, through Sinai to the Promised Land in about 1,500 B.C.

The Greeks grew leeks, and called them *prasa*. In Homer's *Odyssey*, Odysseus returned to Ithaca to find his father Laertes digging under a pear tree, and said to him: 'There is never a plant, neither fig tree nor yet grapevine nor olive nor pear tree nor leek bed uncared for in your garden."

The Roman word for leek was *porrum*. In the days of the Republic, leeks, like onions and garlic, seem to have been regarded as pauper's food. Later, under the emperors, just as Tiberius conceived a passion for cucumbers, so the mad, lyre-playing Nero consumed quantities of leeks in the fond belief that they would improve his singing voice. He was called *porrophagus* or "leek-eater" behind his back: a term of contempt (although, according to Pliny, Nero's lunatic addiction made the leek a fashionable food on Roman dinner tables).

The first-century A.D. gourmand and chef Apicius, under whose name about five hundred

TWO CUNEIFORM TABLETS

YALE BABYLONIAN COLLECTION
*New Haven, U.S.
Dating to 1,700 B.C.,
these tablets reveal a rich
cuisine—the boiled pigeon
recipe includes leeks,
garlic, and aromatic herbs*

recipes were later collected and published in *De Re Coquinaria*, used leeks in several of his sauces. He understood what modern cooks appreciate: that leeks are mucilaginous and act as thickening agents in a sauce.

Did the ancients grow *porrum* leeks, with their thickened stems, undeveloped bulbs, and biennial habit? An Egyptian coffin painting, in the Museo Civico at Bologna, seems to illustrate leek-like *alliums* without swollen bulbs.

Recent research at Fishbourne Palace in West Sussex has indicated that the Romans brought the leek to Britain. *Porrum* leeks are frost-hardy, do not form a bulb, go on growing well into their first winter and can be harvested over a long period, so they are well adapted to northern latitudes. One possible scenario is that, as the plant moved north with the Romans, so varieties were selected for their winter hardiness and long,

Allium porrum

edible leaf bases: somewhat approaching our modern *porrum* leeks, but thinner, with a pronounced bulb.

Leeks were widely grown in northern Europe during the Middle Ages, for cooking and herbal medicine. In 1354, 12 pounds of leek seed was ordered for the King's Palace at Rotherhithe on the Thames, enough to feed an army of guests and retainers, or at any rate to plant up an acre of ground. The usual form was to boil them to death in "pottage," a sort of vegetable stew. A modern equivalent might be Scotch broth, or cock-a-leekie soup.

In the fourteenth century, the Goodman of Paris recommended his wife to use the greasy pot water of pork for boiling leeks, and keep beef or mutton water for boiling cabbages "which should be put on the fire very early in the morning and cooked for a very long time."

There is a much more appealing, modern-sounding recipe for leeks, mixed in a salad with other herbs like parsley, borage and sage, in *The Forme of Cury* [cookbook], a handbook for the cooks of Richard II. "Rinse and wash them clean. Pick them over, pluck them small with thine hands, and mix them well with raw oil. Lay on vinegar and salt and serve it forth."

Leeks, oddly, are conspicuous by their absence in sixteenth-century Dutch or Italian set-piece paintings of grocers' stalls, vegetable markets and still lives, by painters like Valkenborch, Beuckelaer, or Giovanna Garzoni. Other *alliums* such as onions and garlic are regularly featured. In the sixteenth century, Thomas Tusser and John Gerard both spoke of leeks as being commonly cultivated in England. Were they still regarded as paupers'

Now leckes are in season, for pottage ful good, And spareth the milck cow, and purgeth the bloud, These hauing with peason, for pottage in Lent, Thou sparest both otemel and bread to be spent. Thomas Tusser on the Month of March

food, or were they just less popular in continental Europe?

The leek is the national symbol for Welshmen, who wear it in their hats on St. David's Day, March 1st, and at whose expense Shakespeare had a certain amount of fun in *Henry V*. Various explanations have been advanced for the origins of its symbolic use. Welsh soldiers, who fought the English Saxons are believed to have stuck leeks in their helmuts to distinguish friend from foe. The leek is also meant to symbolize the snow of the Welsh mountains and the green of the valleys. All of these suggestions are more or less speculative.

HARVESTING LEEKS FROM A BED

FIFTEENTH CENTURY
Woodcut
from The French Thesaurus

Onion   *Allium cepa of the* Lily *family*

The cultivated onion dates back to prehistoric times. It is mentioned in the Bible, but only once. The Israelites, bored with the manna that "fell with the dew" upon their refugee camp in the Sinai desert, remembered wistfully:

the fish, which we did eat in Egypt freely; the cucumbers, and the melons, and the leeks, and the onions, and the garlick. But now our soul is dried away. There is nothing at all, beside this manna, before our eyes

Numbers 11: 5,6

X

Traces of onion bulbs have been found in Early Bronze Age levels (5,000 B.C.) at Jericho in Palestine, along with fig seeds and date stones. Carvings of onions appear on early Egyptian tombs. Sums spent on feeding laborers on onions and radishes are recorded on one of the Pyramids, built before 3,000 B.C.

Allium cepa is a biennial plant, a member of the Lily family, and a close relation of leeks, chives and garlic. No exact equivalent grows in the wild, but it probably descends from any one of five similar, closely related wild species that still occur in central Asia: *A. oschaninii*, *A. praemixtum*, or *A. pskemense* from the Pamir mountains at the western end of the Tibetan plateau; *A. vavilovii* from the Koppet Dag mountains of Turkmenia; or *A. galanthum* from the Tien Shan mountains on the borders of Russia and China. They all have small bulbs, tall hollow stems that tend to be swollen halfway up, with a distinctive oniony smell (produced by alkyl sulphides) that makes your eyes water.

Perennial plants, they grow in groups on bare, stony ground where other plants do not compete, and sometimes take a decade before they produce their first summer flowers. Pamir villagers dig up *A.pskemense* in the wild and grow it in their gardens, much as onions were domesticated in prehistoric times.

After their first domestication, onion seeds and bulbs were spread by trade—east to India and west to the Mediterranean—and became modified by human selection and the new habitats. The Greeks, Hippocrates (died 430 B.C.) and Theophrastus (332 B.C.), and the Roman writer Pliny the Elder (A.D. 79), were all aware of onions that were flat or round, yellow, red or white, mild or bitter. By medieval times, onions had become a common vegetable throughout Europe. European seafarers took them to Asia, Africa and the New World—it is likely that Columbus planted them in the West Indies in 1494 and they were grown in Massachusetts by 1629. The slave trade played its part: lenghty-storing, high-dry-matter west African cultivars are believed to be the ancestors of the "Creole" onions of Lousiana.

Modern mediterranean onions, white- or silver-skinned, tend to be mild, soft and juicy, though they do not last, or need to, as they can be eaten fresh almost all of the year round. But northern Europe requires a tougher, "winter" cultivar and the onions that appear in sixteenth-century Dutch paintings are probably of this type. "James Keeping," a hardy reddish-brown-skinned winter onion introduced to Britain in the early 1800s by a Mr. James of Lambeth, proved hugely popular for its storage ability. As late as World War II, onion seeds destined for British gardens were still grown abroad, where climatic conditions favored ripening.

Today, onions of the Common Onion group are grown in a variety of shapes and colors. The Japanese onion, a modern cultivar with a yellow skin, is sown in August for early harvesting the following June or July before other onions are ready. Shallots are small onions that divide rapidly and throw off laterals. Their clusters of onions are useful for small-scale cookery, and they keep very well. They, too, have an ancient history. The Greeks and Romans believed they came from Ascalon in Palestine—hence the name "scallions."

The tree or Egyptian onion (*Allium cepa* var. *proliferum*), with two-foot stems bearing small edible bulbs, green at first turning brownish-red, is good for pickling. It was introduced to Britain in 1820 from Canada, where French Canadians called it *"oignon de l'Egypte,"* though there is no evidence of Egyptian origin.

Spring onions, with long leaves and small bulbs, are ordinary *Allium cepa,* planted in the autumn for salad crops the following spring, or in the early spring for harvesting in summer.

The Welsh onion (*Allium fistulosum*) forms a perennial clump, with large, hollow leaves growing from small bulbs. It has nothing to do with Wales; its name derives from the German *welsche,* meaning "foreign," which it is. It descends from *Allium altaicum,* a wild plant from East Kazakhstan and has been cultivated in China and Japan, where it has flavored fried vegetables since prehistoric times. It arrived in western Europe in the 1600s.

In 1998 the world grew thirty-nine million tonnes of dry onions. The USA, Turkey, Iran, India and Japan all produced more than a million tons each, but China was the biggest grower, with ten million tons of dry onions, and 277,000 tons of green onions and shallots.

THE ONION MAN, **1935** *(opposite)*
ARTHUR HAYWARD
1889–1971
Oil on canvas
Leamington Spa Art
Gallery Museum / Warwick
District Council
Warwickshire, U.K.

Asparagus

Asparagus officinalis *of the* Lily *family*

Wild *Asparagus officinalis*, from which our garden asparagus derives, ranges over a huge area centred on the Mediterranean basin: north from Morocco to central Europe and east from Britain to Iran.

You can find it growing on the Steppes of southern Russia and Poland where horses and cattle graze on it like grass; in France by the poplar-lined roadsides; in Britain on sandy ground beside the sea. It is an industrious colonizer and is not fussy about habitat, provided the soil is well drained: riverbanks, limestone cliffs, rubbish tips, churchyards, volcanic hillsides—all are equally welcome.

The asparagus is a perennial plant and each year its underground rhizomes develop feather duster stems up to five feet high, with male and female flowers (small, yellowish or green) usually carried on separate plants. The leaves are like tiny scales on the stems and photosynthesis is carried out by tufts of green, needle like branches (the so-called *cladodes*) in the leaf axils. The red fruits are attractive to birds, particularly blackbirds, thrushes and

pigeons, and become widely dispersed. Any attempt to sort out wild plants from escaped wildings and pinpoint a centre of origin, is pretty much guesswork: its present range, and partiality for salty ground and sea coasts, indicate a Mediterranean origin.

Over the centuries, various subspecies have become adapted to local niches. The horizontal growing, wind-defying *Asparagus officinalis* ssp. *prostratus* is found huddled on the grassy seacliffs and sand dunes of European Atlantic coasts, notably in Cornwall and Pembrokeshire, and has given its name to Asparagus Island off the Lizard. *Acutifolius*, a woody stemmed perennial, scrambles over the dry limestone hillsides of Spain, Greece and Turkey. It has even thinner stems than *officinalis* and hard, thorn-shaped leaves. Its edible spears are strongly flavored, and local people collect them in season.

Today, the thin, primitive (and delicious) spears of gathered asparagus are sold in the markets of southern Europe every spring from April to July—just as they have been since time immemorial.

Who first brought the plant into cultivation and when? The Greeks and Egyptians may have grown asparagus, the Romans certainly did. Galen, the Greek medical writer from Asia Minor who came to Rome to seek his fortune in the second century A.D., referred to it by its Greek name, *asparagos* (the root word *spargao* has lustful, tumescent connotations, and it is easy to see how the connection was made). Marcus ("*Delenda est Carthago*") Cato (234–149 B.C.), rigid disciplinarian both to himself and to his fellow Republicans and the first Roman prose writer of any distinction, wrote in his *De Re Rustica* that it was the only vegetable worth

STILL LIFE OF FRUIT
IN A WICKER BASKET
FRANS SNYDERS
1579–1657
Galerie Goudstikker
Amsterdam
The Netherlands

growing besides cabbages. He implied it was being cultivated and improved in Italy in his day, with considerable success, too, and three centuries later Pliny the Elder (who died in A.D. 79) recorded that three blanched asparagus spears from the Ravenna area could weigh as much as one pound. In the sixteenth century, Venice grew rich from asparagus—among other things—grown on the sands of the Veneto plain, and today the fat, white asparagus, cut below ground level in the Po Valley is eaten all over Italy, and beyond.

According to Pliny's contemporary Columella, who farmed near Cadiz in Spain, the Romans either salted and put up their asparagus in jars of brine and vinegar for later use, or ate them freshly cooked, hot, with a pool of melted butter, pepper and salt, and a squeeze of lemon—much as we do, except that they would have used the precursor of the lemon, the citron. Lemons, unknown to the Romans were a later, Islamic introduction.

It may be no accident that the geographical range of wild *Asparagus officinalis* more or less mirrors the extent of the Roman empire in the age of the Antonines. The Romans planted it like the grape in their distant provinces—even in Britain—and when the Roman Empire receded, colonies of asparagus wildings were left behind.

Its cultivation made a come back with the rise of European monasticism after the Dark Ages. Monks grew it in the herb quarters of their gardens for its culinary and medicinal qualities, along with dill, mint, fennel, parsley, spinach, and rocket: they used its asparagine-containing rhizomes as an aperient, and its fruits as a mild diuretic. In Tudor times it was called *sperage* or *sparage*, and improved cultivars like Violet Dutch were brought over from Holland to plant in the kitchen gardens of great English houses on whose aristocratic dining tables asparagus was highly esteemed.

In the sixteenth century, European artists of still lives and greengrocers' stalls began putting into their pictures bunches of asparagus tied up with raffia, looking just as fat and succulent as the bunches we buy today. Vincenzo Campi, from Cremona in Italy, and Frans Snyders, the Flemish animal painter who collaborated with Rubens, both painted them. Campi's *The Fruit Dealer*, painted before 1591, features a lady proudly displaying her bowls and baskets of mouth-watering autumn fruit and vegetables, including blackberries, globe artichokes, and asparagus, and a plate of plums on top of a pumpkin that can only just recently have been introduced from the New World.

Italy at this time seems to have grown much better asparagus than England, in spite of the

THE FRUIT DEALER

VINCENZO CAMPI

1536–1591

Pinacoteca di Brera

Milan, Italy

ASPARAGUS FROM
FLORE MEDICALE
1814 (opposite)
CHAUMETON
*Lindley Library, Royal
Horticultural Society
London, U.K.*

cross-Channel imports of Dutch cultivars. Giacomo Castelvetro, a teacher and translator on the run from the Inquisition and living in exile in London, complained in 1614 that: "when I see the weedy specimens of this noble plant for sale in London I never cease to wonder why no one has yet taken the trouble to improve its cultivation . . . I am convinced that with the right care you could grow abundant crops of asparagus here with spears as thick as one's middle finger." He described how it was done in Italy: in a trench filled with cattle horns and sieved soil, more horn shavings from comb or posthorn manufacture sprinkled on top, and no cutting for three years after planting. "Whoever reads this little book [*The Fruit, Herbs and Vegetables of Italy*,

written in Italian and privately circulated in manuscript form] should note how the landowners of Verona gave up cultivating flax and wheat some twenty years ago, realizing what large profits could be made from asparagus, and now get three times their yearly income, sending vast quantities as far as Venice, fifty miles away."

In 1667 Samuel Pepys bought a bundle of what he called "sparrow grass" in London's Fenchurch Street for 1s.6d: the old name—"grass" for short—still survives among growers and market traders. When the Huguenots fled France after 1685, they brought with them across the Channel gardening skills that the English did not possess, and planted asparagus fields at

Sandwich in Kent, at Colchester in Essex and at Battersea and Mortlake nearer London.

The Battersea asparagus was rated the earliest and best—by the end of the eighteenth century, more or less on the site of today's Battersea Park in London (begun in 1848), there were 260 acres of mainly asparagus. Mortlake grew another 60 acres. Nowadays, of course, any land that is not park is built over and the asparagus growers have long since decamped to Berkshire, Kent or the Fens.

The main asparagus growing areas of France became the Seine valley near Paris, the central Loire valley, and the delta of the Rhône, and by 1643, Louis XIV's time, forcing beds were used to provide early crops. Brunswick, in the basin of the river Weser, is the ancestral home of German asparagus growing. A popular variety was White German, just like Violet Dutch except that its tips remained milky white an inch or so out of the ground.

Cultivars have not in fact changed that much over the years: Connover's Colossal, a nineteenth-century introduction, is still widely grown, and modern F1 hybrids are only variations on a theme aimed at producing uniformity and vigor out of a seed packet. It has long been recognized, though, that male plants produce better spears: Lucullus, Saxon and Franklin are all modern, all-male cultivars.

Asparagus sailed to the New World with the early settlers, but was not grown there on a commercial scale until the mid-nineteenth century. In the early 1900s a flourishing canning industry for white asparagus developed in the Sacramento to San Joaquin area of California, which is still the premier producer of fresh and canned asparagus in North America.

Corn

Zea mays *of the* Grass *family*

Corn is a planetary food. In 1998, global production was 598 million tons—only two million tons behind and soon to overtake wheat, for years the world's number one food crop. In the last decade alone, production of maize has increased by a startling fifty percent.

Corn (also called maize, sweetcorn, Indian corn, mealies, or corn-on-the-cob) originated in the Americas, that much is certain. But exactly how, when and where is obscure. No exact wild equivalent exists. Archaeologists have found prehistoric traces of corn-like pollen in the Mexico City area dating from about 70,000 years ago, long before men roamed there, let alone built shelters or tilled the soil. Tiny cobs (small and matchbox-sized and dating from about 3,500 B.C.) have also been identified in caves in the Tehuacan valley of Central Mexico. It is believed that a plant of the same genus, *Zea mexicana*—its local name is *Teosinte*—which still grows as an annual, open-ground weed in the mountains of Mexico and Guatemala, may have played a part in its origin. *Teosinte*'s stem is flimsier, and it tillers more, and it lacks a prominent central spike. But it looks rather like corn and hybridizes freely with it. So does another wild, Central American genus, *Tripsacum*, which contains several corn-like species. These, too, may have been possible ancestors.

Nikolai Vavilov, the great Russian botanist who led his students on plant hunting expeditions all over the world in the 1930s and who later died in one of Stalin's labor camps,

believed that corn originated in the Bolivian and Peruvian Andes, then spread to Mexico. Tropical mountains, with microclimates that differ swiftly from level to level made ideal nursery areas for plant mutants (which occur, on average, one in 50,000 times in the natural world), he argued. It was on South America's high spine that corn naturally evolved from a grassy weed into a food plant.

Peruvian Indians first gathered it in the wild, then found it growing in the refuse surrounding their shelters, then cultivated it in garden and farm plots, selecting seed from the best plants. But his claim for an Andean origin is not fully supported by archaeology. Earliest traces of Peruvian corn go back only to around 500 B.C.—two millennia later than the Tehuacan cobs of Mexico.

By the time Columbus arrived, American Indians were growing corn throughout the Americas, from Massachusetts to Argentina. With their crude tools they favoured easily worked, silty river valleys, not the hard, grassy plains of the American corn belt where nearly half the world's production comes from today. Mostly, they slashed and burned: they cleared the forest and grew corn, squash, and beans until weeds and scrub took over. Then the plot

Ol. lith. & pict in Horto Van Houtteano.

million well-fed, well-administered people. Gangs of workmen were engaged in digging terraces and aqueducts, and cutting mountain roads. Inca farmers grew corn in the valleys and, to avoid blight, potatoes in the uplands, and their rulers and priests took part of their crops in tax. Corn and potatoes were the keystones of a thriving culture.

Over the centuries, the American Indians developed five categories of corn: flint (hard-grained) and dent (dimpled-grained) corn for feeding animals and poultry, sweet corn for human eating, pop corn whose kernels exploded under heat into a startling white star shape, and flour corn, soft enough for baking.

When the first settlers arrived in New England, they soon recognised that "Indian corn" (northern flint corn, mostly) was better adapted to the poor soil and short, hot, American summers than any cereal seed they had brought with them. In 1612, Captain John Smith, leader of the Virginian colonists, bartered sixteen bushels of life-giving corn from the Native Americans—and more or less saved the settlement. They had come with cannon and armor and wheat, onion, pea, and bean seeds, but few farming tools and no practical knowledge of how to trap, hunt or fish, still less of how to survive in a wilderness where every strange berry appeared lethal. But they watched the Indian ways, and copied them: they cleared trees and planted corn and boiled and pounded the harvested grains into a paste, and baked them into flat cakes they called "corn pones" (*apones* in the Indian tongue). The surplus they fed to their cattle, pigs and hens, which thrived. When the coastal soil grew too thin to farm, the pioneers used Native American corn, as easily stored and

would be abandoned for a decade until the cycle began again. Sometimes they planted their seed, not in furrows, but, like the Hopi Indians, in holes gradually topped up with soil, or in rows of heaped mounds, bypassing tree stumps too big to be dug out by hand.

Corn filled the granaries of the Toltecs, Aztecs, Mayas and Incas, and powered their empires. When Francisco Pizarro and his small band of men and horses kidnapped the Inca ruler Atahuallpa in 1532, he found himself in control of a vast country, twice the size of Spain, 2,200 miles long, containing nine transported as in Inca days, to fuel their wagons over the Appalachians and down into the rich valley of the Ohio and the bluegrass of Kentucky. On the trail the pioneers ate "journey-cakes" or "johnny-cakes," which were corn pones baked over an open hearth. And how did they summon up the blood? At the end of the eighteenth century, Kentuckians of Bourbon County invented corn alcohol—and bourbon whiskey was born.

Corn is exclusively American. No knowledge of it existed in the Old World before Columbus. Or did it? Overlooking a wildwood glen of the Scottish North Esk river, in Midlothian, stands the romantic chapel of Rosslyn. Scott, Wordsworth and Burns were visitors there, Byron wrote a poem about the adjoining castle and Turner set up his easel on the riverbank below. The Catholic chapel was completed between 1446 and 1484 for William St. Clair, third and last Prince of Orkney and its gloomy interior reveals one of the most extraordinary collections of Gothic stone-carvings to be seen anywhere in western Europe: every available space—walls, pillars, roof, architraves—is decorated with botanical or astronomical motifs, biblical scenes, pagan heads, devils tempting lovers, an angel holding Bruce's heart, portraits of the founder and his master mason—there is even a carved head of the mason's apprentice. Most of the carvings survived the Reformation, and Cromwell too.

If you enter the chapel by the north door, cross to the South Aisle and look up at the window nearest the Lady Chapel, there, over the arch, you will see what looks like a chain of peeled corncobs. Various alternative plants have been proposed—aloe vera or even agave. However, the Indian corn theory fits

intriguingly with the old story, published in 1558 as the *"Zeno Narrative and Map,"* that tells of Henry (the first Prince of Orkney and William St. Clair's grandfather) who led an expedition from Orkney, in 1398, via Shetland and Newfoundland to Nova Scotia, where he wintered with the Micmac Indians. In the spring, so the story goes, Henry set out to return home, but bad weather forced him south and he ran for shelter to the coast of Massachusetts.

The figure of a medieval knight, chiseled out of a rock at Westland, Massachusetts, represents, it is believed, Sir James Gunn of Clyth, one of Henry's companions, who according to the *Zeno Narrative* fell ill and died during their stopover.

Did Prince Henry bring Indian corn home with him, or a drawing of Indian corn? Did his grandson have knowledge of it? Unfortunately, we shall never know. If Henry tried to grow it in Orkney, he would not have had much success, for the Indian varieties needed the hot New England summer to ripen. You can see

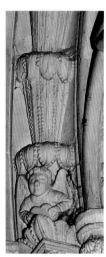

PRE-COLUMBIAN CARVINGS OF CORN

(top and above)

Over south window of Rosslyn Chapel Midlothian, Scotland, U.K.

fields of forage corn grown for dairy cattle in
Scotland today, but these are modern plants,
early-maturing hybrids, developed in the last
decade of the twentieth century.

Corn in the sixteenth century required at
least 120 days of hot summer with reasonable
humidity and a good, drying autumn.
Introduced to Europe, it did well in Turkey,
pushed up the Danube, arrived in Italy as *Grano
Turco*, colonised most of the Mediterranean
littoral, and came to a halt somewhere around
the Dordogne. In 1803, William Cobbett, who
had seen it growing well in America, ate Indian
corn grown on his farm at Botley near
Southampton—but it was regarded as an
unreliable exotic, and did not catch on in
Britain for another 150 years. John Usborne
wrote after World War II:

*I first ate sweet corn at a dinner party in South
Audley Street in August of 1936. It came on in
glorious isolation as an hors-d'oeuvre, like
asparagus, and, like asparagus, accompanied by
melted butter from silver jugs. I felt very strongly
that my hostess, a well-known London society
woman, regarded it as her triumph of the day. It was
certainly for the same reason a memorable day for
me. I had no idea where the corn had been grown;
knowing my hostess, I should not have been surprised
if it had been flown in from the Riviera or by special
plane from the United States . . . I never saw another
ear of sweet corn till September 2nd 1941.*

In the 1800s, corn from the American cornbelt—from Iowa, Nebraska, Illinois, Indiana and Ohio—assumed the same importance for the citizens of the United States as it had once done for the Incas of Peru. It fed their nation—or, more exactly, the nation's animals; nearly all the corn grown on the midwestern farms went for cattle or pig production, or for poultry. Between 1810 and 1910, the continent's population grew from six to ninety-four million, and the pace of increase showed no signs of slowing down. Doomsters predicted the country would starve within a generation. But, by the 1930s, "double-cross hybrid" corn varieties had been developed with astonishing heterosis (the hybrid vigor that Darwin, among others, had identified).

By 1946, on fourteen million fewer acres, twenty-five percent more corn was being grown. America broke all records for the production of corn and soya beans in 1948, and again in 1949 and 1950. Which was just as well, for at that time it was feeding a starving Europe too.

The ghost of Malthus which haunted Europe in the nineteenth century has still not been exorcised. World population has doubled to 5 billion since the 1960s, and is predicted to double again by the 2040s. Should we slash and burn more forests to grow corn, as the Native Americans and European settlers once did? Pour on more spray and fertilizer? The genetic modifiers argue that the new corn crops can be sprayed once, cheaply, with the total weedkiller, glyphosate, while growing; that they can be made resistant to the leaf blight fungus that, in 1970, moved north across the U.S. at the rate of 150 miles a day; that their imported Bt gene kills the corn-borer insect, a major crop reducer in the U.S.

When GM soya beans, largely accepted in America, were imported into Europe in the autumn of 1996, there was an outcry, oddly reminiscent of that which greeted Charles Darwin's nineteenth-century discoveries. We were messing about with something best left to God. Yet nature and man, as Darwin showed, have been selecting and modifying plants—altering "genomes"—for millennia. That is what evolution means. GM corn plants are a step—a long step—along that evolutionary road.

New plants demand, at the very least, careful and sensible assessment. Consider *Zea diploperennis*, a wild relative of corn. Saved from extinction in the very nick of time (its 25-acre niche was due to be slashed and burned within a week), it was discovered in the 1970s on a mountain in the west central state of Jalisco, south of Guadalajara, by a Mexican college student. It is disease-resistant and, uniquely among corn species, perennial. It is hoped and believed that this plant's genes, copied and transferred to farmed plants, will boost production by many millions of tons.

MOCHICA
POTTERY VESSEL,
c. A.D. 300–700
MOCHE, PERU
*British Museum
London, U.K.
A vessel in the form of
three fanged deities
emerging from a bundle of
corncobs*

Index

Credits